Way of Zen
Way of Christ

Satori and the Kingdom of God

by Tony Luke

Published by Tony Luke
Publishing partner: Paragon Publishing, Rothersthorpe
First published 2014
© Tony Luke 2014

ISBN 978-1-78222-350-4

Book design, layout and production management by Into Print
www.intoprint.net
+44 (0)1604 832149

Printed and bound in UK and USA by Lightning Source

Contents

Illustrated with brush drawings by the author

Acknowledgements

The translation of The Gateless Gate and the Zen Stories is that of Nyogen Senzaki and Paul Reps in Zen Flesh, Zen Bones (Charles E. Tuttle Co. Inc. 1957)

Quotations from Master Dogen are taken from Zen is Eternal Life by Roshi P.T.N.H. Jiyu-Kennett (Shasta Abbey Press 1999)

Quotations from the New Testament are from the Revised Standard Version of 1971

Grateful thanks to the community at Throssel Hole Zen Buddhist Abbey in Northumberland for their encouragement, in particular to Rev. Roland for his helpful comments on my manuscript.

Foreword: A personal journey

For me, this book has been a very long time in the making. Much of it has formed part of my spiritual journey for the last 30 years and I have truly longed to get it down on paper, so that others perhaps might be prompted to make similar journeys of discovery to mine. It is my own spiritual journey which leads me, a Christian priest, to write a book on the way of Zen Buddhism and the way of Jesus Christ.

Allow me to describe very briefly something of this journey.

I discovered as a young person that I was never very enamoured of long explanations and always preferred simple images or words of insight. I also found that my personality instinctively preferred poetry to prose, intuition to planning. University threatened for a time to "sort me out." Studying theology at Cambridge encouraged me to think through my faith, ask questions and evaluate everything I was taught. At the same time, university marked my first encounter with religious fundamentalism. I was at first impressed by the keenness, zeal and absolute certainty of some of my evangelical fellow-students. I attended prayer meetings and Bible studies, but was increasingly left with a feeling that they were just far too wordy and that much of what was said was done to impress others and boost our self-esteem.

I was bothered by one fundamental question: "Why do we need to tell God what he already knows?" Surely prayer was about more than that. Turning to the Bible, I was struck

3

afresh by Jesus' teaching on prayer in the Sermon on The Mount: "When you pray, do not heap up empty phrases as the Gentiles do; for they think that they will be heard because of their many words. Do not be like them, for your Father knows what you need before you ask him." (Matt. 6. 7-8) This was a turning-point for me. Or perhaps a turning-back to something I had always instinctively known; that prayer is never truly about words.

After I left university, I worked as a volunteer for a year in a variety of challenging contexts for an organisation called the Church Army. I was asked by them to go on placement in a very traditional, anglo-catholic parish. During this time, I was treated to a weekend away with the young people, which was a silent retreat at an Anglican convent in Norfolk. This was my very first experience of a silent retreat and it felt as though I had at long last discovered something for which I had been unconsciously searching. I discovered the power of sitting in silence. That weekend I felt closer to God and more at peace with myself that I had ever done before and, perhaps, than I have ever done since. It was as though the penny had dropped.

The next year was spent at theological college, where I met regularly with two fellow-students to practise contemplative prayer, using some of the exercises from "The Path of the Mystic" by Peter Spinks and, at the same time, discovering some of the riches of Christian contemplative prayer, devouring the writings of Julian of Norwich, Brother Lawrence, Thomas Merton, Teresa of Avila, Jean-Pierre de

Caussade, the author of The Cloud of Unknowing and many others. The following year, which was the year immediately prior to my ordination, was spent at the Institute of the World Council of Churches near Geneva, where I made a special study of the Eastern Orthodox tradition, learnt about and began to use The Jesus Prayer and, amazingly, for the very first time began to take a serious interest in the writings of faith traditions other than Christianity, an interest which further developed when I began ministry in the multi-cultural city of Derby.

I am ashamed to admit that I cannot for the life of me remember who the distinguished priest was, who led my ordination retreat exactly 30 years ago this year. What I can remember, is that he based the retreat on a book by Henri Nouwen, called "Reaching Out – the three movements of the spiritual life." I was so struck by this book that I purchased a copy there and then. On several occasions Nouwen quotes from another book, entitled "Zen Flesh, Zen Bones" by Paul Reps. I remember thinking what an intriguing title it had! The following summer, whilst on holiday in The Lake District, I spent a rainy hour browsing in a bookshop in Ambleside. I was attracted by the section on Prayer and Spirituality and there, amongst all the other books, was a copy of this very book, "Zen Flesh, Zen Bones." As I read the "101 Zen Stories" and "The Mumonkan or Gateless Gate" translated by Nyogen Senzaki and Paul Reps, I felt as though someone had just awoken me with a slap on the face. I am convinced that if I had not grown up as a Christian and never heard the teachings of Jesus before, they would have had a similar impact, but this was new and fresh and I loved it.

So I discovered Zen in my first year after ordination. During the last thirty years I have both studied, practised and taught meditation and have kept returning again and again to these Zen Buddhist writings. They have walked alongside me during my pastoral ministry as a priest, I have long pondered them and so this book has grown within me over the years; a compelling desire to place the Mumonkan and the teachings of Jesus side by side and allow ourselves to be transformed by them, which is the only reason they were given to us.

A brief introduction to Zen

In the sixth century A.D. an Indian monk named Bodhidharma arrived in China and was presented to the Emperor Wu, who had been a fervent patron of Buddhism. Tradition has it that when the Emperor asked Bodhidharma the highest meaning of the most holy truths, he replied, "Empty, without holiness." At which the Emperor then enquired, "Who is this, who is facing me?" "I don't know," replied Bodhidharma. This style of Buddhism failed to impress the Emperor, and Bodhidharma retreated to a monastery for several years, where he devoted his time to sitting in meditation before a wall and eventually gained a disciple, Hui Ko, who became the second Patriarch of Zen. His teachings were transmitted throughout China under the name of Ch'an Buddhism.

That is the story of the origins of Zen. There are reasons to suspect that this is not the whole story, however, not the least because Zen seems to be thoroughly Chinese in style, having as much affinity to the Taoist and Confucian traditions as to the main streams of Mahayana Buddhism and the Indian philosophy from which it sprung.

The Chinese word *Ch'an*, given to this home-grown branch of Buddhism, comes from the Sanskrit word *dhyana,* or meditation. The essential thesis of Ch'an Buddhism is that the true teaching of the Buddha was not transmitted through the many sutras or collections of the Buddha's sayings, but rather through the practice of *dhyana.*

In the thirteenth century a Japanese monk, Dogen, travelled to China and returned to impart the teachings of Ch'an Buddhism in his native land, particularly through his book, the Shobogenzo. *Ch'an* became in Japan *Zen,* a word which came to describe both the posture for meditation (*zazen* or seated meditation) and the philosophy which surrounded its practice.

Zen is refreshingly direct. Whereas in the main schools of Buddhism enlightenment seems to be a remote prospect, usually reached after many stages and rebirths, in Zen there is an unexpected immediacy. *Satori* (Enlightenment or awakening) can come at any moment, often unexpectedly. Nirvana, far from being a future hope, is seen as a present reality to be discovered. This is especially interesting for Christians, because of the many parallels to Jesus' teaching on the Kingdom of God.

Zen is also astonishingly "unreligious." With its emphasis on "sitting in silence" it therefore sits lightly to any forms of liturgy or ritual. It has few scriptures, is suspicious of long *sutras* and intellectual analysis, and its main writings passed down the generations and collected together take the form of anecdotal stories, short poems and the famous *koans*, those puzzling statements, which are intended to defy reason and open the mind to enlightenment. For this reason, since the days when the first Jesuit priests arrived in Japan from the West, Christians have found little in Zen which cannot be embraced. I would go further than that and say that Christians have much to learn from the simplicity of Zen and its refusal to accept easy answers which do not involve the whole of one's being.

What follows is the most significant collection of koans, the Mumonkan or "Gateless Gate," plus a handful of other classic Zen stories. The Mumonkan, was compiled and commented upon by the Chinese master Ekai, known in Japan as Mumon, in the 12th century. Each of the koans is a barrier to logic, intended to force the student to break through the limited confines of his mind and wake up to a new birth of *satori* or enlightenment.

As Mumon writes in his introduction to the work:

> *The great path has no gates.*
> *Thousands of roads enter it.*
> *When one passes through this gateless gate*
> *He walks freely between heaven and earth.*

There are no answers to the questions of the koans. Each person has to allow them to speak to him or her in their own way and become their own answer, for as they constantly remind us, there is no such thing as second-hand Zen. Therefore, what follows in this book is not a commentary as such, for neither the Zen "koans" nor the parables and teachings of Jesus, which I have attached to them for comparison purposes, are there to be explained or rationalised. However, encouraged by the Master Mumon, who gives guidance for each of the koans, I shall give a rather feeble attempt at providing pointers as to how the koans and the parables have spoken to me and how they might be embraced and made our own. However, if my comments are distracting, feel free to ignore them and allow yourself to be woken up with your own slap to the face, just as I was, when I first encountered the Mumonkan 30 years ago!

The Zen of Christ?

Here is a Zen story:

A university student, while visiting Gasan, asked him: "Have you ever read the Christian Bible?"

"No, read it to me," said Gasan.

The student opened the Bible and read from St.Matthew: "And why take ye thought for raiment? Consider the lilies of the field, how they grow. They toil not, neither do they spin, and yet I say unto you that even Solomon in all his glory was not arrayed like one of these...Therefore take no thought for the morrow, for the morrow shall take thought for the things of itself."

Gasan said: "Whoever uttered those words I consider an enlightened man."

The student continued reading: "Ask and it shall be given you, seek and ye shall find, knock and it shall be opened unto you. For everyone that asketh receiveth, and he that seeketh findeth, and to him that knocketh it shall be opened."

Gasan remarked: "That is excellent. Whoever said that is not far from Buddhahood."

Very few Christians are prepared in the main to be quite as enlightened as Gasan in their estimation of the teachings or teachers of other faith traditions. Sadly, we Christians have tended throughout history to be possessive about our apprehension of the truth and exclusivist in the claims we make about Jesus. I cannot find any justification for this in the teachings of Jesus himself.

It will be clear, I hope, from my comments in this book, that as I have read the Mumonkan and other Zen writings, I have been constantly hearing echoes of the teachings of Jesus at every point. Furthermore, both my study of Zen Buddhism and the practice of meditation have led me to see the teachings of Jesus in a whole new light.

Dom Aelred Graham, in his book "Zen Catholicism", published in 1963 around the time of the Second Vatican Council, puts forward the thesis that the Church has been too concerned with religion **about** Jesus and too little concerned with the religion **of** Jesus. In other words that Christian theology, as it moved into a Hellenistic world, became preoccupied very quickly with the person of Jesus and the doctrines of salvation, at the expense of truly hearing what Jesus was actually teaching about the kingdom of God.

There are similarities between the life and ministry of Jesus and that of Shakyamuni Buddha. Neither are purely mythological figures; they are both grounded in a specific historical context. The ministry of both springs from their self-realisation at about the age of 30: Shakyamuni's awakening to Buddhahood beneath the Bodhi tree and Jesus at his baptism awakening to his true self as The Christ. Both Jesus Christ and Shakyamuni Buddha sought to open up their own transforming experience in a very immediate way to ordinary people, particularly those marginalised by existing religious systems. For this reason their teaching was often regarded as subversive and threatening to those who had reasons to preserve the status quo.

Jesus, in gathering about him a group of disciples with whom he lived, ate and slept was adopting a classic oriental practice, inviting disciples to learn by sharing the common life with the master. An essential part of that practice was the giving of instruction, either through question and answer or through the giving of memorable teaching, which the disciple could take away and use to unlock the truth within themselves. The fact that Jesus' parables and stories were so reliably remembered and written down when he was no longer bodily with them, shows that the intention was that they were also intended to be a resource for future generations and become the "Dharma" of Jesus.

It is not my intention to suggest that the parables and stories of Jesus are in any way identical to the koans and stories of Zen Buddhism, because they are not. Oriental and Hebrew cultures are very different. However, it could be argued that they have more tradition in common than they have with the very dualistic Hellenistic tradition through which much of Christianity came to be expressed as it moved to the West. Westerners particularly find the "shock factor" of some of

Jesus' parables quite puzzling and disconcerting. For example, how could gentle and loving Jesus tell us that we must hate our father and mother and brothers? Anyone familiar with the practice of Zen will know that blunt over-statement is used by the teacher, sometimes accompanied by physical action, to shock the student into realisation. The parable which really highlights this is Jesus' teaching: "It is easier for a camel to go through the eye of a needle, than for a rich man to enter the kingdom of heaven."(Matthew 19.24) I have heard some Christian commentators trying to explain the parable away by saying that there perhaps was a small gate in Jerusalem called the needle-eye, through which camels could not possibly enter! This tries to remove the shock-factor in Jesus' parable, which we know had an effect on those who heard it. They were dismayed, for they had been brought up to believe that riches were a sign of God's blessing and reward. Once we have faced within ourselves the brick-wall of impossibility within the parable, we are ready to really hear the message of grace, that with God all things are possible and the brick-wall disappears. There is something astonishingly Zen-like about this parable. It invites us to overcome the attachment to "self" and come to experience detachment as an act of grace. The parable also contains a measure of humour, for it presents our minds with a ridiculous picture. Dare we believe that Jesus uttered these words with a twinkle in his eye? I would suggest that we have sometimes taken Jesus too seriously and, by attempting to rationalise and systemise his teaching so much, we have missed important dimensions ; the freshness, the joy, the humour and the poetry. My hope and desire in writing this book is that, by placing the koans and other Zen stories and the words of Jesus side by side, we can be encouraged to allow Jesus' words to speak to us in their freshness, setting aside the business of the "mind", namely centuries of Christian doctrinal practice, which can so distract us from hearing the true and authentic "Word" within ourselves, which St.John describes as "the true light which enlightens every human person." (John 1. 9)

The writers of the first three Gospels are quite clear that the essential message of Jesus was the proclamation of the Kingdom of God and the call to repentance:

"Jesus came into Galilee proclaiming the good news of God and saying, 'The time is fulfilled and the kingdom of God is at hand; repent and believe the good news." (Mark 1. 14-15)

Repentance has so often in Christian theology been conceived of in predominantly negative ways, namely, dealing with sin and guilt and turning away from it in order to find forgiveness and a fresh start. The Greek word, "metanoia," means a change of mind, heart and direction with a positive emphasis on what we are turning towards, namely the kingdom of God. Equally, "believe" means far more than intellectual assent. Therefore,"repent and believe the good news," means something like "turn and positively embrace with the whole of your being."

I have heard it said by Christians that Buddhists have no concept of sin. This is untrue. Buddhists are quite clear that the root cause of all the problems of the universe is "delusion", namely the placing of the "false self" or ego-soul at the centre of things, deludedly believing that we are the most important thing and that everything revolves around us. "Satori" or enlightenment/awakening is the freedom from this delusion, which enables us to appreciate and embrace everything as it is in itself, rather than as reflections of our own mind and desires. In Jesus' parables the kingdom of God is something which is discovered, stumbled upon, found within ourselves. It requires the opening of our spiritual eyes to see and, when found, is worth the abandonment of everything else, in order that we might truly enter it. It is also a narrow gate, entering which goes against the inclinations of self, and which can only be achieved by grace, by pure gift. Both Buddhists and Christians believe that the origin of sin lies in a delusion, a falling away from one's true state (whether "image of God" or "Buddha-nature" into the false worship of the self. Repentance means turning back to the source. Jesus constantly invites his disciples to "enter" the kingdom of God; not just to think about it, but to embrace and enter it with the whole of ourselves. The camel in Jesus' parable is akin to the famous ox in Zen Buddhist thinking, which represents the untamed self. The passing through the needle's eye, like entering by the narrow way, speaks of the overcoming of attachment to self, of the need to leave self behind in order to enter the freedom of the Kingdom. When Jesus says "Unless a grain of wheat falls on the ground and dies it remains a single grain, but if it dies it yields a rich harvest," he is echoing what Zen Buddhists refer to as "no self." It is by leaving self behind that we are able to truly find life both for ourselves and for the whole of creation.

Some further things make Zen Buddhist belief and practice particularly pertinent for Christians. The first is the immediacy of enlightenment. In much of Buddhist tradition, enlightenment is seen as a distant goal, usually only achieved after countless lifetimes. Zen begins with the premise that we are all already enlightened, it is only the delusion of self which prevents us from truly realising this. For this reason, "satori" or the realisation of enlightenment is not something which can be worked on, nor is it in any sense a "reward" for perseverance in Buddhist practice. It is rather an unexpected gift, which can occur at the most unlikely moments and there can be countless small awakenings along the way. In a similar way many of Jesus' parables deal with the theme of grace, which is described in terms such as: the growth which happens when we do not expect it; the treasure which is stumbled upon; the way which opens up when everything seems impossible.

We cannot underestimate the importance of the "now" within Zen. Zen teaches that the present moment is all that we have. We waste much of our time and energy either by dwelling in the past through memory or in the future through fantasising about what might be going to happen. The only way out of living either in memory or fantasy is by appreciating the present moment in all its freshness and all things, sentient and non-sentient, in their "suchness." In other words, we are to live each moment as though we had never been there before (which we haven't) and see all things for what they are in themselves, rather than through our own ideas or preconceptions of them. Living each moment with the freshness we see expressed by young children, as they experience the world for the first time, is the way to enlightenment. Does this give us a clue to what Jesus was meaning when he taught us that we had to become like children in order to enter the Kingdom of heaven?

Buddhism is wary of the pitfalls of a dualistic way of thinking. Christianity historically has been full of dualisms, such as heaven/earth, flesh/spirit, divine/human, sacred/secular. For this reason the incarnation has so often been conceptualised in "building-block" terms, an attempt to work out how divinity and humanity can be fitted together within one person. Zen insists on the unity between the absolute and the relative, which offers to Christians a non-dualistic way of understanding incarnation, which is possible precisely because the absolute is always present in the relative, or, to use Christian language, the divine is always present in the human, the sacred in the secular. This not only turns our understanding of the incarnation on its head, but also helps to make sense of the mystical identification between the risen Christ and his followers, expressed through St.Paul's phrases "in Christ" and "the body of Christ" and wonderfully portrayed in Jesus' story about the sheep and the goats: "When did we see you hungry..thirsty..a stranger...naked...sick or in prison? Truly, I tell you, as you did it to the least of these my brethren, you did it to me." (Mathew 25 37-40)

You may wish to keep these themes in mind as we turn to the koans, stories and scriptures. They need to be approached in a meditative way and I will make some suggestions in the next chapter as to how the book might be used. As I explained earlier, Zen "koans" are not just mental riddles to be solved. Despite my comments upon them, they cannot be "solved" by the mind. There are no answers. They can only be "solved" by making the whole self the subject and the answer of the koan. Can we dare to apply a similar meditative discipline to Jesus teachings? Are we able to truly listen with the whole of ourselves and "enter" with the whole of ourselves? That is the challenge presented by Zen and it is most importantly the challenge of Jesus, if we truly have ears to hear what he is saying.

How to use this book – the practice of zazen

The reader may be excused for thinking that what follows on from this chapter makes for a rather unusual book. For the comments on the Mumonkan and extracts from the Gospels are not written with the purpose of engaging in intellectual argument or of exploring doctrines, either Buddhist or Christian; rather they arise out of the experience of meditation and need to be read and explored in that same spirit. It was not my intention to write a book that should be read from cover to cover. I hope that the reader will wish to keep returning both to the koans and to Jesus' words and use them as a basis for meditation.

Zazen or "sitting meditation" is the essential heart of Zen Buddhist practice and is undoubtedly the greatest gift which Zen gives to Christians and to the world community.

The most important thing is to find a time, place and a posture, where one can sit as still as possible. I find the best time for meditation is first thing in the morning, when the mind is fresh and the house is quiet, but, of course, time can be found for meditation at any time of the day. The best location is a quiet, uncluttered room, especially where there is space to sit comfortably on the floor. It is important to sit relaxed but alert with a straight back. Traditionally this was achieved by sitting in the lotus or half-lotus positions, supported by a zafu or round cushion. For most westerners this is really difficult, if not impossible, so the use of a meditation bench to support the pelvis is usually a much better option. Equally there is no problem with doing effective meditation on an upright chair, preferably with a wedged cushion to tip the pelvis forwards and so straighten the back. When sitting on a chair, the feet need to be flat to the floor, so a person with short legs may need a chair with shorter legs or something to support the feet. Whilst sitting, the left hand should be placed palm upwards on top of the right hand with the thumbs gently touching each other, both hands resting on the lap just in front of the abdomen. The spine needs to be held comfortably, not stiffly, erect. A good way of achieving this is to sway the body from side to side a few times rather like a pendulum coming to rest and to imagine an invisible puppet-string pulling upwards from the top of the head. The shoulders should be in line with the ears. The mouth should be closed with the tip of the tongue lightly touching the top of the mouth behind the teeth. Zen teaches meditating with eyes half-open, so as not to induce sleep or dreaminess. The eyes should not focus on anything in particular but rest on a point on the ground a short distance in front of the body. Before settling the hands for meditation, I find it helpful to focus my mind and body by doing the traditional "gassho", which is placing the palms of my hands together with the finger-tips almost touching my nose and the forearms straight and not resting on my chest. While sitting, I then perform a forward bow with the whole of my upper body. Physically-speaking, it is a good way of opening the vertebrae before sitting still in meditation.

When your posture is comfortable but alert, the best way to focus the mind and body is to concentrate for a few moments on your breathing. Start by simply observing the breath as it enters and leaves your body. Then gradually allow those breaths to become longer and slower, paying particular attention to the outbreath, allowing it to become an unspoken sigh, a letting go of all tensions and tightness in the mind and body and any thoughts which may be chasing around in the mind. A good way of doing this is to visualise, when breathing in, that the breath is being taken right to the top of the head. Pause slightly before the outbreath and then visualise the outbreath cascading down the spine from the top of the head to the base of the body. Then pause again slightly after exhalation before breathing in again. After repeating this breathing exercise a few times, take your attention away from the breathing, allow the body to breathe naturally and focus your mind's attention on the silence around and within, the silence which is before, after and behind any noises which may come to your ears. The purpose of meditation is not to block your thoughts and senses. Our natural tendency, when a thought comes into our heads is to follow it and engage in a train of thought, rather like a puppy follows yapping at the heels of a passer-by. Rather, we should adopt the stance of someone watching at a window, who observes a passer-by and lets them continue on their way. There is a world of difference between noticing someone pass by and letting them simply pass by, than immediately engaging in mind-dialogue, such as, "That's Mr. So-and-so and he lives in such a place and do your remember when he said......" This is a healthy way to approach the thoughts which will come to our mind during meditation. We should observe them, gently let them go and re-focus, rather than hitching a ride on them! If re-focussing is particularly difficult, you can return to the breathing-observation exercise until the mind is stilled.

The Soto Zen school teaches the value of zazen or "simply sitting" in itself with nothing more added, for the mind is its own koan. It is the older Rinzai school of Zen which taught the use of koans in meditation, given by the master to the trainee. I have found it valuable to take a key word from the koans or the parables and to repeat it slowly in my head, usually in time with the outbreath, allowing the word to permeate my mind and body. Equally, repeating one of the short phrases slowly, focussing on a word at a time can be a very effective way of entering into what is truly being said, rather than seeing whole sentences together as an intellectual, mind-exercise. The koans, for instance, are not puzzles to be solved by the intellect. For example, the first koan, "Joshu's dog" is an invitation to turn away from intellectual speculation about Buddha nature and allow the phrase "Mu"(No-thing, No-self) to become so much part of you, that you are Mu and Mu is you. Or taking a phrase of Jesus, "Enter by the narrow gate," really hear and respond with the whole of your being to the invitation contained in the word "enter", sense the focus and diligent application implied by the word "narrow" and the opening up of oneself to enter into fullness of life, which the word "gate" represents. However, be mindful that words and phrases, however simple, can lead us into mind games and, when we find this is happening, we will need to re-focus and return to simply sitting in silence.

I include here some awareness exercises, which I have used over the years to relax and focus the mind and body for meditation:

Pore breathing

Having done the preliminary breathing exercise outlined above, visualise with the outbreath that you are breathing out of every pore on the surface of your skin. Begin this exercise with the top of your head, imagining that you are breathing out through the surface of the scalp and the root of your hair. As you breathe out, let go of any tightness or tension by tensing the appropriate part of the body and then relaxing it on the outbreath (This is particularly important with the forehead, jawline, shoulders, abdomen, fingers and toes, parts of our bodies where tension is often focussed.) From the top of the head move to the forehead, then gradually move around your body via the cheeks, the jawline, the back of the neck, the shoulders, the chest and the abdomen. When you move onto the limbs, visualise that outbreath cascading down into the abdomen and then trickling down through the legs and arms, leaving the body through the fingertips and toes. When you have completed this exercise, you should be very aware of your body, relaxed but alert, and of the space it occupies. It is then possible to enlarge that awareness so that there is no distinction between the body and what is beyond it. All is one.

Fingertip centring

Begin by lifting your hands from your lap and placing them the same distance apart as the width of your body with the palms facing each other. This usually works best if you tuck your elbows into the sides of your body, so that your arms are parallel. You can do the full "pore breathing" exercise as above or move straight to your arms, visualising that the outbreath flows down the arms and out through the fingertips. Pay particular attention to the fingertips and be aware of the surface of the fingertips and the sensations there. Very gradually, a millimetre or two at a time, begin to move the palms closer together, focussing your mind's attention on the space enclosed by your two hands. Allow at least five minutes or more for your hands to draw closer together and as they get closer do not allow them to touch. Keep the fingertips and palms about a centimetre apart and be aware of the still but energised space between them. Maintain the focus of your attention on that still space. When you are ready, allow the hands to return to the lap, but maintain your mind's attention on the still space in front of you, where the hands once were. The next step, when you are ready, is to take that still centre inside yourself, somewhere in the chest area, and maintain the focus of your mind there.

Canvas of sounds

After one of the preliminary breathing exercises, focus your attention on the sounds in the world around you. Don't follow the sounds around with your mind, just observe them, let them go and move on. Set yourself the task of hearing all the sounds, the background or momentary sounds as well as the obvious, persistent ones. Don't forget to listen to internal sounds connected with your own body. After a period of listening with awareness, change the focus of your listening to the silence, which is present before, after and behind the sounds; the canvas on which the sounds are painted. Listen to the silence around and within. All is one.

Sky mind

I usually find this works best with the eyes only very slightly open. Visualise the sky on a bright day; vast, endless, full of light. Then visualise that sky all around you like a limitless sphere of light, above, beneath, behind, on all sides with your mind at the centre. Then allow yourself to disappear, so that there is just sky, just light and you are that sky, that light extending infinitely in all directions. All is one.

Walking Meditation

This is a traditional Zen practice, used between lengthy periods of zazen. Maintaining an erect posture, with the hands clasped gently in front of the chest, you walk slowly, your eyes focussed straight ahead, but your mind's attention resting on the walking. Each foot should be raised and lowered slowly with all the awareness of balance you would require if walking on a tightrope or beam, rather than on the floor. Walking meditation is good for developing a positive awareness, which can be continued when you come to sit.

Mantra walking

This is a useful way of meditating when walking at normal speed anywhere. Walk at your normal pace, but time the outbreath to coincide with every fourth step. Combine the outbreath with a word, uttered soundlessly from the heart. You can then take three steps on the inbreath and breath out on the fourth to create a natural rhythm: Word, 2, 3, 4, Word, 2, 3, 4, Word, 2, 3, 4.....

As you persevere, take heart from the kindly words of Master Dogen:

"Forget the selfish self for a little and allow the mind to remain natural for this is very close to the Mind that seeks the Way."

The Gateless Gate

and the Gospels

"The great path has no gates,

Thousands of roads enter it.

When one passes through this gateless gate

He walks freely between heaven and earth."

(Mumon)

"Enter by the narrow gate;

For the gate is wide and the way is easy, that leads to destruction,

And those who enter by it are many.

For the gate is narrow and the way is hard, that leads to life,

And those who find it are few."

(Jesus)

1. Joshu's Dog

A monk asked Joshu, a Chinese Zen master: "Has a dog Buddha-nature or not?" Joshu answered: "Mu."

[Mu is the negative symbol in Chinese, meaning "No thing"]

Mumon's comment: To realize Zen one has to pass through the barrier of the patriarchs. Enlightenment always comes after the road of thinking is blocked. If you do not pass the barrier of the patriarchs or if your thinking road is not blocked, whatever you think, whatever you do, is like a tangling ghost. You may ask: What is a barrier of a patriarch? This one word, Mu, is it. This is the barrier of Zen. If you pass through it you will see Joshu face to face. Then you can work hand in hand with the whole line of patriarchs. Is this not a pleasant thing to do? If you want to pass this barrier, you must work through every bone in your body, through every pore of your skin, filled with this question: What is Mu? and carry it day and night. Do not believe it is the common negative symbol meaning nothing. It is not nothingness, the opposite of existence. If you really want to pass this barrier, you should feel like drinking a hot iron ball that you can neither swallow nor spit out. Then your previous lesser knowledge disappears. As a fruit ripening in season, your subjectivity and objectivity naturally become one. It is like a dumb man who has had a dream. He knows about it but he cannot tell it. When he enters this condition his ego-shell is crushed and he can shake the heaven and move the earth. He is like a great warrior with a sharp sword. If a Buddha stands in his way, he will cut him down; if a patriarch offers him any obstacle, he will kill him; and he will be free in his way of birth and death. He can enter any world as if it were his own playground. I will tell you how to do this with this koan: Just concentrate your whole energy into this Mu, and do not allow any discontinuation. When you enter this Mu and there is no discontinuation, your attainment will be as a candle burning and illuminating the whole universe

Has a dog Buddha-nature?
This is the most serious question of all.
If you say yes or no,
You lose your own Buddha-nature.

My comment: The answer is neither "yes" nor "no", for intellectual answers are useless. With Mu we are invited to enter into a greater reality, to become "Mu", where the subject and the object become one. "No thing" is not the same as "nothing", but we are invited by it to throw away all the useless knowledge and ways of thinking we have acquired up to now. This is the gateway to all the koans; coming with an emptiness. As Mumon says, "it is not nothingness, the opposite of existence," rather it is the very essence of existence. Therefore the initial question about the dog is superceded by a greater reality, before which "previous lesser knowledge disappears." The answer is simply to let go and to be. Entering Mu is to discover that all things are oneself and one is all things and you awaken to the reality that all creatures are Buddha's life, including incidentally the dog.

Jesus says: "Do not be anxious about your life...Is not life more than food, and the body more than clothing?... Do not be anxious about tomorrow, for tomorrow will be anxious for itself ." (Matthew 6. 25, 34)

My comment: As well as letting go of idle speculations, we must also let go of those anxieties which kill abundant living. We cannot change the past, nor control the future, but we can *live* in the present moment. We must be prepared to let go of all that we cling to.

2. Hyakujo's Fox

Once when Hyakujo delivered some Zen lectures an old man attended them, unseen by the monks. At the end of each talk when the monks left so did he. But one day he remained after they had gone, and Hyakujo asked him: "Who are you?" The old man replied: "I am not a human being, but I was a human being when the Kashapa Buddha preached in this world. I was a Zen master and lived on this mountain. At that time one of my students asked me whether or not the enlightened man is subject to the law of causation. I answered him: 'The enlightened man is not subject to the law of causation.' For this answer evidencing a clinging to absoluteness I became a fox for five hundred rebirths, and I am still a fox. Will you save me from this condition with your Zen words and let me get out of a fox's body? Now may I ask you: Is the enlightened man subject to the law of causation?" Hyakujo said: "The enlightened man is one with the law of causation." At the words of Hyakujo the old man was enlightened. "I am emancipated," he said, paying homage with a deep bow. "I am no more a fox, but I have to leave my body in my dwelling place behind this mountain. Please perform my funeral as a monk." Then he disappeared. The next day Hyakujo gave an order through the chief monk to prepare to attend the funeral of a monk. "No one was sick in the infirmary," wondered the monks. "What does our teacher mean?" After dinner Hyakujo led the monks out and around the mountain. In a cave, with his staff he poked out the corpse of an old fox and then performed the ceremony of cremation. That evening Hyakujo gave a talk to the monks and told them this story about the law of causation. Obaku, upon hearing the story, asked Hyakujo: "I understand that a long time ago because a certain person gave a wrong Zen answer he became a fox for five hundred rebirths. Now I want to ask: If some modern master is asked many questions and he always gives the right answer, what will become of him?" Hyakujo said: "You come here near me and I will tell you." Obaku went near Hyakujo and slapped the teacher's face with his hand, for he knew this was the answer his teacher intended to give him. Hyakujo clapped his hands and laughed at this discernment. "I thought a Persian had a red beard," he said, "and now I know a Persian who has a red beard."

Mumon's comment: "The enlightened man is not subject." How can this answer make the monk a fox? "The enlightened man is one with the law of causation." How can this answer make the fox emancipated? To understand this clearly one has to have just one eye.

Controlled or not controlled?
The same dice shows two faces.
Not controlled or controlled,
Both are a grievous error.

My comment: "The enlightened man is not subject" has the effect of placing him apart, making him a special case. The truly enlightened is neither removed from causation nor carried along by it – he is one with it; he is both cause and effect. The koan invites us to move beyond right and wrong answers. Nor does it matter whether you are a monk or a fox. What matters is to be what you are. To be enlightened is to be neither bound nor free, controlled or uncontrolled, but one new reality; therefore having "one eye" not two.

Jesus says: "If you continue in my word, you are truly my disciples, and you will know the truth, and the truth will make you free... If the Son makes you free, you will be free indeed." (John 8. 31, 32, 36)

My comment: Not controlled or uncontrolled but free to be one's true self.

3. Gutei's Finger

Gutei raised his finger whenever he was asked a question about Zen. A boy attendant began to imitate him in this way. When anyone asked the boy what his master had preached about, the boy would raise his finger. Gutei heard about the boy's mischief. He seized him and cut off his finger. The boy cried and ran away. Gutei called and stopped him. When the boy turned his head to Gutei, Gutei raised up his own finger. In that instant the boy was enlightened. When Gutei was about to pass from this world he gathered his monks around him. "I attained my finger-Zen," he said, "from my teacher Tenryu, and in my whole life I could not exhaust it." Then he passed away.

Mumon's comment: Enlightenment, which Gutei and the boy attained, has nothing to do with a finger. If anyone clings to a finger, Tenryu will be so disappointed that he will annihilate Gutei, the boy, and the clinger all together.

Gutei cheapens the teaching of Tenryu,
Emancipating the boy with a knife.
Compared to the Chinese god who pushed aside a
mountain with one hand
Old Gutei is a poor imitator.

My comment: One cannot imitate or copy another's Zen; you have to live it for yourself. The boy was at fault for copying Gutei and believing that was what was required. Gutei **is** his finger in that by his finger he demonstrates his Zen, his true self and allows his body to speak more powerfully than words can. The boy is just a mimic. He needs to learn that no-one else's truth can be his truth. The intensity of his pain and Gutei's command to stop frees him from this delusion for he had become the pain, he was feeling it at first hand.

Jesus' finger Zen: "This they said to test him, that they might have some charge to bring against him. Jesus bent down and wrote with his finger upon the ground. And as they continued to ask him, he stood up and said to them, 'Let him who is without sin among you be the first to throw a stone at her.' And once more he bent down and wrote with his finger on the ground." (John 8. 6-8)

My comment: How well Jesus understood that the language of his body and of silence was more powerful than words.

Jesus says: " The kingdom of heaven is like a merchant in search of fine pearls, who, on finding one pearl of great value, went and sold all that he had and bought it." (Matthew 13. 45)

My comment: There are no short-cuts or half-solutions to finding the kingdom of God. Like Gutei's finger, we cannot settle for half-measures, for it is worth our all, our everything.

4. A Beardless Foreigner

Wakuan complained when he saw a picture of bearded Bodhidharma: "Why hasn't that fellow a beard?"

Mumon's comment: If you want to study Zen, you must study it with your heart. When you attain realization, it must be true realization. You yourself must have the face of the great Bodhidharma to see him. Just one such glimpse will be enough. But if you say you met him, you never saw him at all.

One should not discuss a dream
In front of a simpleton.
Why has Bodhidharma no beard?
What an absurd question!

My comment: How we tend to dwell on externals! Instead we should be seeking the true "face" of Bodhidharma. Bearded or beardless does not matter. Bodhidharma's face is your face.

Jesus says: "Beware of practising your piety in front of men in order to be seen by them.; for then you will have no reward from your Father in heaven...When you fast, anoint your head and wash your face, that your fasting may not be seen by men but by your Father, who is in secret." (Matthew 6. 1, 17,18)

My comment: How often do we concentrate on externals, on the "face" we present to the world? Rather, we should concentrate on the "inner face" we present in secret to God. Our true face is God's face in whose image each of us is made.

5. Kyogen Mounts the Tree

Kyogen said: "Zen is like a man hanging in a tree by his teeth over a precipice. His hands grasp no branch, his feet rest on no limb, and under the tree another person asks him: 'Why did Bodhidharma come to China from India?' "If the man in the tree does not answer, he fails; and if he does answer, he falls and loses his life. Now what shall he do?"

Mumon's comment: In such a predicament the most talented eloquence is of no use. If you have memorized all the sutras, you cannot use them. When you can give the right answer, even though your past road was one of death, you open up a new road of life. But if you cannot answer, you should live ages hence and ask the future Buddha, Maitreya.

Kyogen is truly a fool
Spreading that ego-killing poison
That closes his pupils' mouths
And lets their tears stream from their dead eyes.

My comment: If a person clings onto life, he knows not Zen. Enlightenment comes through detachment, letting go, through the death of the ego.

Jesus says: "Whoever seeks to gain his life will lose it, and he whoever loses his life will find it." (Luke 17. 33)

6. Buddha Twirls a Flower

When Buddha was in Grdhrakuta mountain he turned a flower in his fingers and held it before his listeners. Every one was silent. Only Maha-Kashapa smiled at this revelation, although he tried to control the lines of his face. Buddha said: "I have the eye of the true teaching, the heart of Nirvana, the true aspect of non-form, and the ineffable stride of Dharma. It is not expressed by words, but especially transmitted beyond teaching. This teaching I have given to Maha-Kashapa."

Mumon's comment: Golden-faced Gautama thought he could cheat anyone. He made the good listeners as bad, and sold dog meat under the sign of mutton. And he himself thought it was wonderful. What if all the audience had laughed together? How could he have transmitted the teaching? And again, if Maha-Kashapa had not smiled, how could he have transmitted the teaching? If he says that realization can be transmitted, he is like the city slicker that cheats the country dub, and if he says it cannot be transmitted, why does he approve of Maha-Kashapa?

At the turning of a flower
His disguise was exposed.
No one in heaven or earth can surpass
Maha-Kashapa's wrinkled face.

My comment: The true Dharma, the true teaching is transmitted without words. The twirling of the flower in itself means nothing, for the Buddha teaches with his very being. All words are inadequate. The smile of Maha-Kashapa shows that the learning is intuitive, not reasoned by the mind.

Jesus says: "He who has ears to hear, let him hear.... To you it has been given to know the secrets of the kingdom of God; but for others they are in parables, so that seeing they may not see, and hearing they may not understand." (Luke 8. 8,10)

"The Word became flesh and dwelt among us, full of grace and truth.." (John 1. 14)

My comment: This statement of Jesus shows how the purpose of the parables is so often misunderstood by Christians. How often we have been taught that Jesus used simple illustrations in order to help people to understand. The parables, however, like the koans, are not there to explain but to awaken. It is possible to hear the words and see Jesus speaking them and yet still not have woken up to perceive the kingdom of God. As with Buddha, the kingdom of God is revealed by Jesus' very being.

7. Joshu Washes the Bowl

A monk told Joshu: "I have just entered the monastery. Please teach me." Joshu asked: "Have you eaten your rice porridge?" The monk replied: "I have eaten." Joshu said: "Then you had better wash your bowl." At that moment the monk was enlightened.

Mumon's comment: Joshu is the man who opens his mouth and shows his heart. I doubt if this monk really saw Joshu's heart. I hope he did not mistake the bell for a pitcher.

It is too clear and so it is hard to see.
A dunce once searched for a fire with a lighted lantern.
Had he known what fire was,
He could have cooked his rice much sooner.

My comment: The monk has just entered the monastery and wants to be taught. His first lesson is that of "being", do the normal tasks in the right spirit. He expects instruction, but needs instead to learn by humble practice. Like him, we make the mistake of assuming that instruction comes from the outside. Our learning is within us and there is no such thing as Zen divorced from the life we are actually living in the present moment. Now is the moment.

Jesus says: "Not everyone who says to me, 'Lord, Lord,' shall enter the kingdom of heaven, but he who does the will of my Father in heaven." (Matthew 7. 21)

"Who then is the faithful and wise servant, whom his master has set over his household, to give them their food at the proper time? Blessed is that servant whom his master, when he comes, will find so doing.....Watch therefore, for you know neither the day nor the hour." (Matthew 24.45-46, 25.13)

My comment: How often our words of devotion are belied by our outward behaviour and inner intentions. Those who came to Jesus full of themselves are sent away to find humility and faithfully submit to God's will. Jesus bids us live each moment and perform the tasks of each moment in the light of his coming.

8. Keichu's Wheel

Getsuan said to his students: "Keichu, the first wheel-maker of China, made two wheels of fifty spokes each. Now, suppose you removed the nave uniting the spokes. What would become of the wheel? And had Keichu done this, could he be called the master wheel-maker?"

Mumon's comment: If anyone can answer this question instantly, his eyes will be like a comet and his mind like a flash of lightning.

When the hubless wheel turns,
Master or no master can stop it.
It turns above heaven and below earth,
South, north, east, and west.

My comment: The wheel is the turning universe. The koan is an invitation to become one with the wheel of creation. The hub is removed because you yourself must lose the false self, about which you falsely believe all things revolve. What would become of the wheel? You would become the wheel and the wheel would become you. Like Keichu you are a master wheel-maker, for you have achieved self-realisation.

Jesus says: "The eye is the lamp of the body. So, if your eye is sound, your whole body will be full of light; but if your

eye is not sound, your whole body will be full of darkness."
(Matthew 6. 22,23)

My comment: Where do we place our focus, not of the physical eye, but of the inner eye of the spirit. Focus on light and our whole selves will be filled with light.

9. A Buddha before History

A monk asked Seijo: "I understand that a Buddha who lived before recorded history sat in meditation for ten cycles of existence and could not realize the highest truth, and so could not become fully emancipated. Why was this so?" Seijo replied: "Your question is self-explanatory." The monk asked: "Since the Buddha was meditating, why could he not fulfill Buddhahood?" Seijo said: "He was not a Buddha."

Mumon's comment: I will allow his realization, but I will not admit his understanding. When one ignorant attains realization he is a saint. When a saint begins to understand he is ignorant.

It is better to realize mind than body.
When mind is realized one need not worry about body.
When mind and body become one
The man is free. Then he desires no praising.

My comment: Enlightenment is not a reward for endurance or persistence in meditation, therefore time alone cannot create a Buddha from one who is not. Enlightenment is gift, not a reward for self-effort.

Jesus says: "Truly I say to you, it will be hard for a rich man to enter the kingdom of heaven. It is easier for a camel to go through the eye of a needle than for a rich man to enter the

46

kingdom of God. ..With men this is impossible, but with God all things are possible."

My comment: The parables of the kingdom focus on the grace, the generous underserved gift of God. The encounter with a rich young man prompted Jesus' teaching. You cannot buy or earn your way into the kingdom of God. To do this is like a camel trying to push through the eye of the needle. Entering the kingdom is an underserved gift, for with God the impossible becomes possible.

10. Seizei Alone and Poor

A monk named Seizei asked of Sozan: "Seizei is alone and poor. Will you give him support?" Sozan asked: "Seizei?" Seizei responded: "Yes, sir." Sozan said: "You have Zen, the best wine in China, and already have finished three cups, and still you are saying that they did not even wet your lips."

Mumon's comment: Seizei overplayed his hand. Why was it so? Because Sozan had eyes and knew with whom to deal. Even so, I want to ask: At what point did Seizei drink wine?

The poorest man in China,
The bravest man in China,
He barely sustains himself,
Yet wishes to rival the wealthiest.

My comment: How can someone be poor, who is rich beyond measure? If Zen is the best wine in China, he cannot yet have drunk it or he would know that he was rich.

Jesus says: "Seek first the kingdom of God and his righteousness, and all things shall be yours as well." (Matthew 6. 33)

"Blessed are you poor, for yours is the kingdom of God." (Luke 6. 20)

My comment: Those who seem to possess nothing, truly possess everything.

11. Joshu Examines a Monk in Meditation

Joshu went to a place where a monk had retired to meditate and asked him: "What is, is what?" The monk raised his fist. Joshu replied: "Ships cannot remain where the water is too shallow." And he left. A few days later Joshu went again to visit the monk and asked the same question. The monk answered the same way. Joshu said: "Well given, well taken, well killed, well saved." And he bowed to the monk.

Mumon's comment: The raised fist was the same both times. Why is it Joshu did not admit the first and approved the second one? Where is the fault? Whoever answers this knows that Joshu's tongue has no bone so he can use it freely. Yet perhaps Joshu is wrong. Or, through that monk, he may have discovered his mistake. If anyone thinks that the one's insight exceeds the other's, he has no eyes.

The light of the eyes is as a comet,
And Zen's activity is as lightning.
The sword that kills the man
Is the sword that saves the man.

My comment: Was the first answer the correct one or not? There is no objective way of knowing. The monk's answer remained constant, despite Joshu's apparent scorn, therefore the monk was confident in his Zen; his self-realisation did not need any external approval. "The monk answered in the same way." He has become "What is" and truly answered Joshu in himself.

Jesus says: "Beware of practising your piety before men in order to be seen by them; for then you will have no reward from your Father in heaven." (Matthew 6. 1)

My comment: Jesus warns about the pitfalls of seeking external approval.

12. Zuigan Calls His Own Master

Zuigan called out to himself every day: "Master." Then he answered himself: "Yes, sir." And after that he added: "Become sober." Again he answered: "Yes, sir." "And after that," he continued, "do not be deceived by others." "Yes, sir; yes, sir," he answered.

Mumon's comment: Old Zuigan sells out and buys himself. He is opening a puppet show. He uses one mask to call "Master" and another that answers the master. Another mask says "Sober up" and another, "Do not be cheated by others." If anyone clings to any of his masks, he is mistaken, yet if he imitates Zuigan, he will make himself fox-like.

Some Zen students do not realize the true man in a mask
Because they recognize ego-soul.
Ego-soul is the seed of birth and death,
And foolish people call it the true man.

My comment: Zuigan cannot let go of the ego-soul. By approving of himself with "Yes, sir", he considers himself higher than the others, who might deceive him. Is he not the one who is deceiving himself? The masks of ego-soul, which he wears, hides his true nature, which he cannot reveal either to the world or to himself; hence the complex mind games he plays.

Jesus says: "Truly, I say to you, unless you turn and become like little children, you will never enter the kingdom of heaven. Whoever humbles himself like this child, he is the greatest in the kingdom of heaven." (Matthew 18. 4)

"He who is greatest among you must be your servant; whoever exalts himself will be humbled, and whoever humbles himself will be exalted." (Matthew 23. 11)

My comment: Jesus teaches the way of humility, which necessitates a letting-go of the ego-soul in order to discover the true self, hidden in God.

13. Tokusan Holds His Bowl

Tokusan went to the dining room from the meditation hall holding his bowl. Seppo was on duty cooking. When he met Tokusan he said: "The dinner drum is not yet beaten. Where are you going with your bowl?" So Tokusan returned to his room. Seppo told Ganto about this. Ganto said: "Old Tokusan did not understand ultimate truth." Tokusan heard of this remark and asked Ganto to come to him. "I have heard," he said, "you are not approving my Zen." Ganto admitted this indirectly. Tokusan said nothing. The next day Tokusan delivered an entirely different kind of lecture to the monks. Ganto laughed and clapped his hands, saying: "I see our old man understands ultimate truth indeed. None in China can surpass him."

Mumon's comment: Speaking about ultimate truth, both Ganto and Tokusan did not even dream it. After all, they are dummies.

Whoever understands the first truth
Should understand the ultimate truth.
The last and first,
Are they not the same?

My comment: Ganto shows himself to be foolish and far from the spirit of Zen, as he seeks to score points and jostle for position. How can Ganto make a judgement on another's understanding of ultimate truth? He is unable to admit his criticism openly, therefore he is far from being honest. By returning to his room and by altering his lecture, Tokusan demonstrates that there is no "ultimate truth", no final expression, no last word to end all words. He is undefensive, because he does not have any ego-soul to defend. He accepts the transitory, changing ebb and flow of all things and lives with it.

Jesus says: "Judge not, that you be not judged. For with the judgement you pronounce you will be judged, and the measure you give will be the measure you get. Why do you see the speck that is in your brother's eye, but do not notice the log that is in your own eye?" (Matthew 7. 1-3)

My comment: When we pass judgement upon another, we are actually seeking to distance ourselves from those features of our ego-soul, which we see in another person, but prefer not to recognise in ourselves. We seek to put others down, in order to build ourselves up. Therefore in judging, we are actually judging ourselves. If we truly know ourselves, we will not be so hasty to judge. When we refuse to judge we are enabled to let go of the ego-soul. This abandonment of ego-soul and therefore of judgement is superbly acted out for us by Jesus in the story of the woman taken in adultery (John 8) and in the words on the cross, "Father forgive them, for they do not know what they are doing." (Luke 23. 34)

14. Nansen Cuts the Cat in Two

Nansen saw the monks of the eastern and western halls fighting over a cat. He seized the cat and told the monks: "If any of you say a good word, you can save the cat." No one answered. So Nansen boldly cut the cat in two pieces. That evening Joshu returned and Nansen told him about this. Joshu removed his sandals and, placing them on his head, walked out. Nansen said: "If you had been there, you could have saved the cat."

Mumon's comment: Why did Joshu put his sandals on his head? If anyone answers this question, he will understand exactly how Nansen enforced the edict. If not, he should watch his own head.

Had Joshu been there,
He would have enforced the edict oppositely.
Joshu snatches the sword
And Nansen begs for his life.

My comment: The quarrelling monks show that they still live dualistically, with division and faction. Nansen's killing of the cat is an attempt to waken the monks up to their situation, to save them. When we live with division, we are cut into pieces like the cat. He invites us to see ourselves as the cat. Joshu's actions are indeed the "good word" spoken without words, which show that he has passed beyond dualism. For him there is no head and feet, hats and sandals, up or down. His apparent folly demonstrates his liberation. He has passed from death to life.

Jesus says: "Truly, truly I say to you, unless a grain of wheat falls into the earth and dies, it remains alone; but if it dies it bears much fruit." (John 12. 24)

My comment: Jesus, by his death, wants to wake us up to our situation and save us. He invites us to pass with him from death to life.

15. Tozan's Three Blows

Tozan went to Ummon. Ummon asked him where he had come from. Tozan said: "From Sato village." Ummon asked: "In what temple did you remain for the summer?" Tozan replied: "The temple of Hoji, south of the lake." "When did you leave there?" asked Ummon, wondering how long Tozan would continue with such factual answers. "The twenty-fifth of August," answered Tozan. Ummon said: "I should give you three blows with a stick, but today I forgive you." The next day Tozan bowed to Ummon and asked: "Yesterday you forgave me three blows. I do not know why you thought me wrong." Ummon, rebuking Tozan's spiritless responses, said: "You are good for nothing. You simply wander from one monastery to another." Before Ummon's words were ended Tozan was enlightened.

Mumon's comment: Ummon fed Tozan good Zen food. If Tozan can digest it, Ummon may add another member to his family. In the evening Tozan swam around in a sea of good and bad, but at dawn Ummon crushed his nut shell. After all, he wasn't so smart. Now, I want to ask: Did Tozan deserve the three blows? If you say yes, not only Tozan but every one of you deserves them. If you say no, Ummon is speaking a lie. If you answer this question clearly, you can eat the same food as Tozan.

The lioness teaches her cubs roughly;

The cubs jump and she knocks them down.
When Ummon saw Tozan his first arrow was light;
His second arrow shot deep.

My comment: Tozan is rebuked for his factual answers, which dwell on external circumstances, located in space and time. Ummon's questions regarding where he had come from and in what temple he remained have a deeper meaning. His wandering from "one monastery to another" indicates Tozan's spiritual state. He is looking for constant re-assurance, hence his concern as to whether Ummon thinks his responses good or bad. It is this dependence upon the opinions of others which makes Ummon say "You are good for nothing." The truly enlightened person does not come and go, he simply "is."

Jesus says: "Let what you say be simply "Yes" or "No"; anything more than this comes from evil." (Matthew 5. 37)

My comment: Jesus teaches that the true disciple must have an inner integrity and self-honesty, which is not swayed by external circumstances or the demands of the false self.

16. Bells and Robes

Ummon asked: "The world is such a wide world, why do you answer a bell and don ceremonial robes?"

Mumon's comment: When one studies Zen one need not follow sound or colour or form. Even though some have attained insight when hearing a voice or seeing a colour or a form, this is a very common way. It is not true Zen. The real Zen student controls sound, colour, form, and actualizes the truth in his everyday life. Sound comes to the ear, the ear goes to sound. When you blot out sound and sense, what do you understand? While listening with ears one never can understand. To understand intimately one should see sound.

When you understand, you belong to the family;
When you do not understand, you are a stranger.
Those who do not understand belong to the family,
And when they understand they are strangers.

My comment: The crucial words are "answer" and "don", which suggest an attachment to sound, colour, form and external things, especially to the immediate familiar things, such as a bell or a robe. The familiar and the material can be dangerous. Zen does not seek to "blot out sound and sense, but rather to transcend the immediate and realise a oneness with the "wide world", including all sound, colour and form.

Jesus says: "Do not lay up for yourselves treasures on earth...but lay up for yourselves treasures in heaven...For where your treasure is, there will your heart be also." (Matthew 6. 19-21)

My comment: Where is our "treasure" and where is our "heart?"

17. The Three Calls of the Emperor's Teacher

Chu, called Kokushi, the teacher of the emperor, called to his attendant: "Oshin." Oshin answered: "Yes." Chu repeated, to test his pupil: "Oshin." Oshin repeated: "Yes." Chu called: "Oshin." Oshin answered: "Yes." Chu said: "I ought to apologize to you for all this calling, but really you ought to apologize to me."

Mumon's comment: When old Chu called Oshin three times his tongue was rotting, but when Oshin answered three times his words were brilliant. Chu was getting decrepit and lonesome, and his method of teaching was like holding a cow's head to feed it clover. Oshin did not trouble to show his Zen either. His satisfied stomach had no desire to feast. When the country is prosperous everyone is indolent; when the home is wealthy the children are spoiled. Now I want to ask you: Which one should apologize?

When prison stocks are iron and have no place for the head, the prisoner is doubly in trouble.
When there is no place for Zen in the head of our generation, it is in grievous trouble.
If you try to hold up the gate and door of a falling house,
You also will be in trouble.

My comment: The threefold calling and answering of Chu and Oshin simply serves to demonstrate their pride and stubbornness. If either had been practising Zen, there would be no need for three calls and three answers; the first call would have sufficed.

Jesus says: "But many that are first will be last, and the last first." (Matthew 19. 30)

18. Tozan's Three Pounds

A monk asked Tozan when he was weighing some flax: "What is Buddha?" Tozan said: "This flax weighs three pounds."

Mumon's comment: Old Tozan's Zen is like a clam. The minute the shell opens you see the whole inside. However, I want to ask you: Do you see the real Tozan? Three pounds of flax in front of your nose, Close enough, and mind is still closer. Whoever talks about affirmation and negation Lives in the right and wrong region.

My comment: The question, "What is Buddha?" is an absurd question. Buddha is all things and Buddha is no-thing. Buddha **is**. Buddha is not to be found by speculations of the mind. Buddha is to be found by truly living the present moment, in which Tozan is weighing flax, therefore his answer is more appropriate than many.

Jesus says: "Have I been with you so long, and yet you do not know me? He who has seen me has seen the Father; how can you say, 'Show us the Father?' Do you not believe that I am in the Father and the Father in me?" (John 14. 9-10)

"For judgement I came into this world, that those who do not see may see, and that those who see may become blind." (John 9. 39)

My comment: "Seeing" the presence of God is of far more importance than speculation or words.

19. Everyday Life Is the Path

Joshu asked Nansen: "What is the path?" Nansen said: "Everyday life is the path." Joshu asked: "Can it be studied?" Nansen said: "If you try to study, you will be far away from it." Joshu asked: "If I do not study, how can I know it is the path?" Nansen said: "The path does not belong to the perception world, neither does it belong to the nonperception world. Cognition is a delusion and noncognition is senseless. If you want to reach the true path beyond doubt, place yourself in the same freedom as sky. You name it neither good nor not-good." At these words Joshu was enlightened.

Mumon's comment: Nansen could melt Joshu's frozen doubts at once when Joshu asked his questions. I doubt though if Joshu reached the point that Nansen did. He needed thirty more years of study.

In spring, hundreds of flowers; in autumn, a harvest moon;
In summer, a refreshing breeze; in winter, snow will accompany you.
If useless things do not hang in your mind,
Any season is a good season for you.

My comment: Life is to be lived. The path has to be walked. It can neither be rationalised nor avoided. In this lies true freedom, "the freedom of the sky." Go with the flow. Keep walking; keep living.

Jesus says: "Ask, and it shall be given you; seek and you will find; knock and it will be opened to you. For everyone who asks receives, and he who seeks finds, and to him who knocks it shall be opened."

My comment: Do not give up. Keep walking. Keep seeking.

20. The Enlightened Man

Shogen asked: "Why does the enlightened man not stand on his feet and explain himself?" And he also said: "It is not necessary for speech to come from the tongue."

Mumon's comment: Shogen spoke plainly enough, but how many will understand? If anyone comprehends, he should come to my place and test out my big stick. Why, look here, to test real gold you must see it through fire.

If the feet of enlightenment moved, the great ocean would overflow;
If that head bowed, it would look down upon the heavens.
Such a body has no place to rest. . . .
Let another continue this poem.

My comment: The life of the enlightened man speaks for itself. Put it into words and it is lost for good. Simply "be."

Jesus says: "The kingdom of God does not come in such a way as to be seen. No-one will say, "Look, here it is!" or, "There it is!"; because the kingdom of God is within you." (Luke 17. 20-21)

My comment: So often we expect the kingdom of God to be revealed by external signs. Instead we must open ourselves to receive it and discover it within.

21. Dried Dung

A monk asked Ummon: "What is Buddha?" Ummon answered him: "Dried dung."

Mumon's comment: It seems to me Ummon is so poor he cannot distinguish the taste of one food from another, or else he is too busy to write readable letters. Well, he tried to hold his school with dried dung. And his teaching was just as useless.

Lightning flashes,
Sparks shower.
In one blink of your eyes
You have missed seeing.

My comment: What is Buddha? Answer this and you have missed the point. Answer this and you are left not with Buddha but with dried dung, something useless. Any answer is dried dung. But can we become the "dung", even as we wish to become Buddha? Can we recognise the poverty of our nature and become the "dung" or the "shit-stick", as some translations put it?

Jesus says: "So you also, when you have done all that is commanded you, say. 'We are unworthy servants; we have only done what was our duty.'" (Luke 16. 10)

"And an argument arose among them as to which was the greatest. But when Jesus perceived the thought of their hearts, he took a child and put him by his side, and said to them, 'Whoever receives this child in my name receives me, and whoever receives, receives the one who sent me; for he who is least among you all is the one who is great.'" (Luke 9. 46-48)

My comment: Jesus teaches us the way of humility. To be the Christ, you must first be the servant, the child, the least.

22. Kashapa's Preaching Sign

Ananda asked Kashapa: "Buddha gave you the golden-woven robe of successorship. What else did he give you?" Kashapa said: "Ananda." Ananda answered: "Yes, brother." Said Kashapa: "Now you can take down my preaching sign and put up your own."

Mumon's comment: If one understands this, he will see the old brotherhood still gathering, but if not, even though he has studied the truth from ages before the Buddhas, he will not attain enlightenment.

The point of the question is dull but the answer is intimate.
How many persons hearing it will open their eyes?
Elder brother calls and younger brother answers,
This spring does not belong to the ordinary season.

My comment: What is the true legacy of the Buddha? This is a fundamental question of Zen. The true legacy of the Buddha cannot be transmitted by external things.

Jesus says: "I am with you always, even to the end of time." (Matthew 28. 20)

My comment: The true legacy of Christ is not words or teachings but eternal presence.

23. Do Not Think Good, Do Not Think Not-Good

When he became emancipated the sixth patriarch received from the fifth patriarch the bowl and robe given from the Buddha to his successors, generation after generation. A monk named E-myo out of envy pursued the patriarch to take this great treasure away from him. The sixth patriarch placed the bowl and robe on a stone in the road and told E-myo: "These objects just symbolize the faith. There is no use fighting over them. If you desire to take them, take them now." When E-myo went to move the bowl and robe they were as heavy as mountains. He could not budge them. Trembling for shame he said: "I came wanting the teaching, not the material treasures. Please teach me." The sixth patriarch said: "When you do not think good and when you do not think not-good, what is your true self?" At these words E-myo was illumined. Perspiration broke out all over his body. He cried and bowed, saying: "You have given me the secret words and meanings. Is there yet a deeper part of the teaching?" The sixth patriarch replied: "What I have told you is no secret at all. When you realize your own true self the secret belongs to you." E-myo said: "I was under the fifth patriarch many years but could not realize my true self until now. Through your teaching I find the source. A person drinks water and knows himself whether it is cold or warm. May I call you my teacher?" The sixth patriarch replied: "We studied together under the fifth patriarch. Call him your teacher, but just treasure what you have attained."

Mumon's comment: The sixth patriarch certainly was kind in such an emergency. It was as if he removed the skin and seeds from the fruit and then, opening the pupil's mouth, let him eat.

You cannot describe it, you cannot picture it,
You cannot admire it, you cannot sense it.
It is your true self, it has nowhere to hide.
When the world is destroyed, it will not be destroyed.

My comment: Buddhahood, the knowledge of the true self cannot be described, pictured, sensed, taught or learnt. It cannot be discovered by mental process. "Do not think," says the sixth patriarch. So often we define ourselves by external principles, by self-affirmation (thinking good) or self-denial (thinking not-good) The true self is realised in the simple act of being. This is the secret treasure E-myo attained.

Jesus says: The kingdom of heaven is like treasure hidden in a field, which a man found and covered up. He is so happy that he goes and sells everything he has and buys that field." (Matthew 13. 44)

My comment: The kingdom of heaven is not something which is taught or learnt or inherited from others. The man happened to find the treasure, as though he stumbled upon it. Discovery of God's kingdom is God's gift.

24. Without Words, Without Silence

A monk asked Fuketsu: "Without speaking, without silence, how can you express the truth?" Fuketsu observed: "I always remember springtime in southern China. The birds sing among innumerable kinds of fragrant flowers."

Mumon's comment: Fuketsu used to have lightning Zen. Whenever he had the opportunity, he flashed it. But this time he failed to do so and only borrowed from an old Chinese poem. Never mind Fuketsu's Zen. If you want to express the truth, throw out your words, throw out your silence, and tell me about your own Zen.

Without revealing his own penetration,
He offered another's words, not his to give.
Had he chattered on and on,
Even his listeners would have been embarrassed.

My comment: As Mumon says, "Tell me about your own Zen." Expressing our own Zen is more eloquent than either words or silence.

Jesus says: "A sound tree cannot bear evil fruit, nor can a bad tree bear good fruit...Thus you will know them by their fruits." (Matthew 7. 18,20)

"A good man out of the good treasure of his heart produces good." (Luke 6. 45)

My comment: What is expressed by my life?

25. Preaching from the Third Seat

In a dream Kyozan went to Maitreya's Pure Land. He recognized himself seated in the third seat in the abode of Maitreya. Someone announced: "Today the one who sits in the third seat will preach." Kyozan arose and, hitting the gavel, said: "The truth of Mahayana teaching is transcendent, above words and thought. Do you understand?"

Mumon's comment: I want to ask you monks: Did he preach or did he not? When he opens his mouth he is lost. When he seals his mouth he is lost. If he does not open it, if he does not seal it, he is 108,000 miles from truth.

In the light of day,
Yet in a dream he talks of a dream.
A monster among monsters,
He intended to deceive the whole crowd.

My comment: Kyozan makes a grave mistake. He dreams himself as a great teacher, pointing the ignorant to the way of truth. When he says "Do you understand?" he contradicts himself. How can you understand what is beyond words or thought? If truth is beyond words or thought, how can you preach it? It is not a matter of understanding, but of living.

Jesus says: You are the light of the world. A city set on a hill cannot be hid. Nor do men light a lamp and put it under a bushel. Let your light so shine before men, that they may see your good works and give glory to your Father who is in heaven." (Matthew 5. 14-16)

My comment: A radiant life is the most eloquent sermon.

26. Two Monks Roll Up the Screen

Hogen of Seiryo monastery was about to lecture before dinner when he noticed that the bamboo screen lowered for meditation had not been rolled up. He pointed to it. Two monks arose from the audience and rolled it up. Hogen, observing the physical moment, said: "The state of the first monk is good, not that of the other."

Mumon's comment: I want to ask you: Which of those two monks gained and which lost? If any of you has one eye, he will see the failure on the teacher's part. However, I am not discussing gain and loss.

When the screen is rolled up the great sky opens,
Yet the sky is not attuned to Zen.
It is best to forget the great sky
And to retire from every wind.

My comment: Does Zen end when the meditation screen is rolled up? Hogen's Zen does not continue. If his Zen continued in his lecture, he would not have been so swift to judge.

Jesus says: "Judge not, and you will not be judged; condemn not, and you will not be condemned; forgive, and you will be forgiven; give, and it will be given to you; good measure, pressed down, shaken together, running over, will be put into your lap. For the measure you give, will be the measure you get back." (Luke 6. 37,38)

27. It Is Not Mind, It Is Not Buddha, It Is Not Things

A monk asked Nansen: "Is there a teaching no master ever preached before?" Nansen said: "Yes, there is." "What is it?" asked the monk. Nansen replied: "It is not mind, it is not Buddha, it is not things."

Mumon's comment: Old Nansen gave away his treasure-words. He must have been greatly upset.

Nansen was too kind and lost his treasure.
Truly, words have no power.
Even though the mountain becomes the sea,
Words cannot open another's mind.

My comment: As soon as Nansen opens his mouth, he imparts second-hand teaching. The "teaching no master ever preached before", cannot be preached with words. What is this teaching without preaching? Each must discover his own teaching (never preached before) through Mu – no-thing, the way of detachment.

Jesus says: "What is the kingdom of God like? And to what shall I compare it? It is like a grain of mustard-seed, which a man took and sowed in his garden; and it grew and became a tree, and the birds of the air made nests in its branches." (Luke 13. 18,19)

My comment: The person sowed the seed of the kingdom in **his** garden, therefore the tree which grows is peculiar to each person, a tree which has never grown in that way before.

28. Blow Out the Candle

Tokusan was studying Zen under Ryutan. One night he came to Ryutan and asked many questions. The teacher said: "The night is getting old. Why don't you retire?" So Tokusan bowed and opened the screen to go out, observing: "It is very dark outside." Ryutan offered Tokusan a lighted candle to find his way. Just as Tokusan received it, Ryutan blew it out. At that moment the mind of Tokusan was opened. "What have you attained?" asked Ryutan. "From now on," said Tokusan, "I will not doubt the teacher's words." The next day Ryutan told the monks at his lecture: "I see one monk among you. His teeth are like the sword tree, his mouth is like the blood bowl. If you hit him hard with a big stick, he will not even so much as look back at you. Someday he will mount the highest peak and carry my teaching there." On that day, in front of the lecture hall, Tokusan burned to ashes his commentaries on the sutras. He said: "However abstruse the teachings are, in comparison with this enlightenment they are like a single hair to the great sky. However profound the complicated knowledge of the world, compared to this enlightenment it is like one drop of water to the great ocean." Then he left that monastery.

Mumon's comment: When Tokusan was in his own country he was not satisfied with Zen although he had heard about it. He thought: "Those Southern monks say they can teach Dharma outside of the sutras. They are all wrong. I must teach them." So he traveled south. He happened to stop near Ryutan's monastery for refreshments. An old woman who was there asked him: "What are you carrying so heavily?" Tokusan replied: "This is a commentary I have made on the Diamond Sutra after many years of work." The old woman said: "I read that sutra which says: 'The past mind cannot be held, the present mind cannot be held, the future mind cannot be held.' You wish some tea and refreshments. Which mind do you propose to use for them?" Tokusan was as though dumb. Finally he asked the woman: "Do you know of any good teacher around here?" The old woman referred him to Ryutan, not more than five miles away. So he went to Ryutan in all humility, quite different from when he had started his journey. Ryutan in turn was so kind he forgot his own dignity. It was like pouring muddy water over a drunken man to sober him. After all, it was an unnecessary comedy.

A hundred hearings cannot surpass one seeing,
But after you see the teacher, that one glance cannot surpass a hundred hearings.
His nose was very high
But he was blind after all.

My comment: A lesson in humility. Tokusan begins with his "nose very high" and asks so many questions, because he expects there to be answers which will satisfy him. Ryutan invites him to embrace the darkness of not-knowing, of which blowing out the candle is a visible demonstration. Therefore Tokusan burns his commentaries on the sutras,; those things which weigh him down, which he "carries so heavily." He humbles himself and embraces the path of not-knowing. Knowing so much, he was blind. Knowing nothing, he can see.

Jesus says: "For judgement I came into this world, that those who do not see may see, and that those who see may become blind." (John 9.39)

"Truly, truly I say to you, unless one is born anew, he cannot see the kingdom of God." (John 3. 3)

29. Not the Wind, Not the Flag

Two monks were arguing about a flag. One said: "The flag is moving." The other said: "The wind is moving." The sixth patriarch happened to be passing by. He told them: "Not the wind, not the flag; mind is moving."

Mumon's comment: The sixth patriarch said: "The wind is not moving, the flag is not moving. Mind is moving." What did he mean? If you understand this intimately, you will see the two monks there trying to buy iron and gaining gold. The sixth patriarch could not bear to see those two dull heads, so he made such a bargain.

Wind, flag, mind moves,
The same understanding.
When the mouth opens
All are wrong.

My comment: A question of subjectivity and objectivity. The mind registers that the flag moves. The mind interprets from that that the wind moves. Ultimately, wind, flag and mind are all one movement.

Jesus says: "Look at the fig-tree, and all the trees; as soon as they come out in leaf, you see for yourselves and know that the summer is very near. So also, when you see these things taking place, you know that the kingdom of God is near." (Luke 21. 29-31)

My comment: Jesus invites us to read the signs and truly see the kingdom of God. It is possible for the mind to simply register these things without seeing the reality which lies behind them.

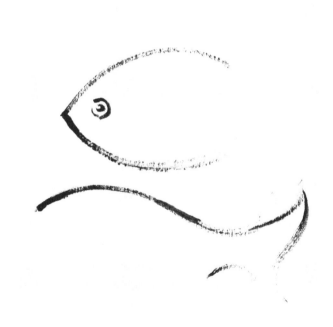

30. This Mind Is Buddha

Daibai asked Baso: "What is Buddha?" Baso said: "This mind is Buddha."

Mumon's comment: If anyone wholly understands this, he is wearing Buddha's clothing, he is eating Buddha's food, he is speaking Buddha's words, he is behaving as Buddha, he is Buddha. This anecdote, however, has given many a pupil the sickness of formality. If one truly understands, he will wash out his mouth for three days after saying the word Buddha, and he will close his ears and flee after hearing "This mind is Buddha."

Under blue sky, in bright sunlight,
One need not search around.
Asking what Buddha is
Is like hiding loot in one's pocket and declaring oneself innocent.

My comment: This mind is Buddha, but Buddha is more than this mind. Baso trots out his answer parrot-fashion like a learned dogma. Hence Mumon's injunction to wash out our mouths and close up our ears whenever we try to express truth in words, lest we think we have found the answer by repeating a standard phrase like, "This mind is Buddha."

Jesus says: "'Who do you say that I am?' And Peter answered , 'You are the Christ of God.' But he charged them to tell this to no-one, saying, 'The Son of Man must suffer many things, and be rejected by the elders and chief priests ans scribes, and be killed, and on the third day be raised.'"

My comment: Peter formulates in words his faith in Jesus. Jesus knows by these words alone that he has not yet found the answer. He tries to lead his disciples understanding onwards to perceive something which goes beyond the stock phrase, "You are the Christ, the Messiah."

31. Joshu Investigates

A traveling monk asked an old woman the road to Taizan, a popular temple supposed to give wisdom to the one who worships there. The old woman said: "Go straight ahead." When the monk proceeded a few steps, she said to herself: "He also is a common church-goer." Someone told this incident to Joshu, who said: "Wait until I investigate." The next day he went and asked the same question, and the old woman gave the same answer. Joshu remarked: "I have investigated that old woman."

Mumon's comment: The old woman understood how war is planned, but she did not know how spies sneak in behind her tent. Old Joshu played the spy's work and turned the tables on her, but he was not an able general. Both had their faults. Now I want to ask you: What was the point of Joshu's investigating the old woman?

When the question is common
The answer is also common.
When the question is sand in a bowl of boiled rice
The answer is a stick in the soft mud.

My comment: The difference lies in the intention. The monk is searching for the temple, as though wisdom were to be found outside oneself. Therefore he interprets the woman's direction in a physical sense and behaves like all temple-goers. Joshu imitates the monk, but neither his question nor the woman's response have the same intention. "Go straight ahead" is an instruction to continue along the same spiritual path, which will lead to the spiritual temple of enlightenment.

Jesus says: "Enter by the narrow gate; for the gate is wide and the way is easy, that leads to destruction, and those who enter by it are many. For the gate is narrow and the way is hard, that leads to life, and those who find it are few."

My comment: In this most Zen-like teaching of Jesus, he warns us to avoid the crowded common path and seek and find that narrow path, which is peculiar to each person.

32. A Philosopher Asks Buddha

A philosopher asked Buddha: "Without words, without the wordless, will you tell me truth?" The Buddha kept silence. The philosopher bowed and thanked the Buddha, saying: "With your loving kindness I have cleared away my delusions and entered the true path." After the philosopher had gone, Ananda asked the Buddha what he had attained. The Buddha replied: "A good horse runs even at the shadow of the whip."

Mumon's comment: Ananda was the disciple of the Buddha. Even so, his opinion did not surpass that of outsiders. I want to ask you monks: How much difference is there between disciples and outsiders?

To tread the sharp edge of a sword,
To run on smooth-frozen ice,
One needs no footsteps to follow.
Walk over the cliffs with hands free.

My comment: Why ask the Buddha, when the answer is inside oneself? Hence the Buddha keeps silence. The philosopher realises what the Buddha is revealing to him. Ananda, though supposedly a disciple, misses the point by asking for information. The Buddha teaches without teaching, that each person must find his or her own path. Hence Mumon's comment: "One needs no footsteps to follow." In this there is no difference between disciple and outsider.

Jesus says: "And men will come from east and west, and from north and south, and sit at table in the kingdom of God. And behold. Some are last who will be first, and some are first who will be last." (Luke 13. 29-30)

My comment: There is no difference between disciple and outsider. All can find their way to the kingdom of God. Those who think they have arrived, may be far off, and those who think they are far off, may be nearer than they think.

33. This Mind Is Not Buddha

A monk asked Baso: "What is Buddha?" Baso said: "This mind is not Buddha."

Mumon's comment: If anyone understands this, he is a graduate of Zen.

If you meet a fencing-master on the road, you may give him your sword,
If you meet a poet, you may offer him your poem.
When you meet others, say only a part of what you intend.
Never give the whole thing at once.

My comment: There is no answer in words to the question, "What is Buddha?" Anything answered with the mind will always fall short of the truth. Therefore we can say with confidence like Baso, "This mind is not Buddha," even if we cannot say what Buddha is.

34. Learning Is Not the Path

Nansen said: "Mind is not Buddha. Learning is not the path."

Mumon's comment: Nansen was getting old and forgot to be ashamed. He spoke out with bad breath and exposed the scandal of his own home. However, there are few who appreciate his kindness.

When the sky is clear the sun appears,
When the earth is parched rain will fall.
He opened his heart fully and spoke out,
But it was useless to talk to pigs and fish.

My comment: Both of these koans reinforce that the way to Buddha-hood is not through the mind, i.e. words or concepts or learning. The way is through letting go of "Mind."

35. Two Souls

"Seijo, the Chinese girl," observed Goso, "had two souls, one always sick at home and the other in the city, a married woman with two children. Which was the true soul?"

Mumon's comment: When one understands this, he will know it is possible to come out from one shell and enter another, as if one were stopping at a transient lodging house. But if he cannot understand, when his time comes and his four elements separate, he will be just like a crab dipped in boiling water, struggling with many hands and legs. In such a predicament he may say: "Mumon did not tell me where to go!" but it will be too late then.

The moon above the clouds is the same moon,
The mountains and rivers below are all different.
Each is happy in its unity and variety.
This is one, this is two.

My comment: This koan calls upon us to recognise the essential unity of all things. The "true soul" is one with everything.

Jesus says: "May they all be one; even as you, Father, are in me, and I in you, may they also be in us." (John 17.21)

"Truly, I say to you, as you did it to one of the least of these my brethren, you did it to me." (Matthew 25. 40)

36. Meeting a Zen Master on the Road

Goso said: "When you meet a Zen master on the road you cannot talk to him, you cannot face him with silence. What are you going to do?"

Mumon's comment: In such a case, if you can answer him intimately, your realization will be beautiful, but if you cannot, you should look about without seeing anything.

Meeting a Zen master on the road,
Face him neither with words nor silence.
Give him an uppercut
And you will be called one who understands Zen.

My comment: It is self-consciousness, which causes us to ask in advance, 'What shall I say? What shall I do?' The answer is simply to "be."

Jesus says: "Do not be anxious beforehand what you are to say; but say whatever is given you in that hour." (Mark 13. 11)

My comment: The answer is simply to "trust."

37. A Buffalo Passes Through the Enclosure

Goso said: "When a buffalo goes out of his enclosure to the edge of the abyss, his horns and his head and his hoofs all pass through, but why can't the tail also pass?"

Mumon's comment: If anyone can open one eye at this point and say a word of Zen, he is qualified to repay the four gratifications, and, not only that, he can save all sentient beings under him. But if he cannot say such a word of true Zen, he should turn back to his tail.

If the buffalo runs, he will fall into the trench;
If he returns, he will be butchered.
That little tail
Is a very strange thing.

My comment: Enlightenment requires the whole-hearted gift of oneself, the complete embracing of no-thing in order to discover one's true self. The tail is that bit of ourselves we hold back from surrendering. It represents the fear of letting go, which has to be transcended.

Jesus says: He who loves Father and mother more than me is not worthy of me; and he who does not take his cross and follow me is not worthy of me. He who finds his life will lose it, and he who loses his life for my sake will find it." (Matthew 10. 37-39)

My comment: Jesus calls us to nothing less than a whole-hearted surrender of ourselves, that we might truly discover ourselves.

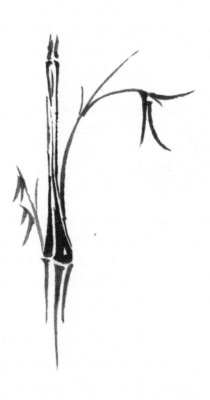

38. An Oak Tree in the Garden

A monk asked Joshu why Bodhidharma came to China. Joshu said: "An oak tree in the garden."

Mumon's comment: If one sees Joshu's answer clearly, there is no Shakyamuni Buddha before him and no future Buddha after him.

Words cannot describe everything.
The heart's message cannot be delivered in words.
If one receives words literally, he will be lost,
If he tries to explain with words, he will not attain enlightenment in this life.

My comment: Joshu refuses to give an answer with words. There is no answer with words. There is no objective answer. The answer lies within oneself. Discover in oneself what made Bodhidharma come to China. Then you will be like the oak tree in the garden, which does not reflect on its existence or try to put it into words, rather it simply "is" an oak tree standing in the garden.

Jesus says: "The kingdom of heaven is like yeast which a woman took and hid in three measures of flour, until all was leavened." (Matthew 13. 33)

My comment: The kingdom of God is not about believing the right things or saying the right things, but about allowing your life to be leavened by the presence of the kingdom of God, which works away silently and unseen.

39. Ummon's Sidetrack

A Zen student told Ummon: "Brilliancy of Buddha illuminates the whole universe." Before he finished the phrase Ummon asked: "You are reciting another's poem, are you not?" "Yes," answered the student. "You are sidetracked," said Ummon. Afterwards another teacher, Shishin, asked his pupils: "At what point did that student go off the track?"

Mumon's comment: If anyone perceives Ummon's particular skillfulness, he will know at what point the student was off the track, and he will be a teacher of man and Devas. If not, he cannot even perceive himself.

When a fish meets the fishhook
If he is too greedy, he will be caught.
When his mouth opens
His life already is lost.

My comment: Zen can never be second-hand; you cannot copy another. The student tries to sound enlightened by quoting something which sounds profound. He merely reveals that he has second-hand Zen and therefore is on a sidetrack. The most important thing is to be yourself.

Jesus says: "Beware of false prophets, who come to you in sheep's clothing but inwardly are ravenous wolves."

(Matthew 7. 15) "You have heard that it was said, 'You shall love your neighbour and hate your enemy.' But I say to you, Love your enemies and pray for those who persecute you." (Matthew 5. 43)

My comment: Jesus bids us beware of those who seem to say and do the right things, but whose intention is far from good. He also demonstrates his own originality, rather than just re-iterating the tradition of his forefathers.

40. Tipping Over a Water Vase

Hyakujo wished to send a monk to open a new monastery. He told his pupils that whoever answered a question most ably would be appointed. Placing a water vase on the ground, he asked: "Who can say what this is without calling its name?" The chief monk said: "No one can call it a wooden shoe." Isan, the cooking monk, tipped over the vase with his foot and went out. Hyakujo smiled and said: "The chief monk loses." And Isan became the master of the new monastery.

Mumon's comment: Isan was brave enough, but he could not escape Hyakujo's trick. After all, he gave up a light job and took a heavy one. Why, can't you see, he took off his comfortable hat and placed himself in iron stocks.

Giving up cooking utensils,
Defeating the chatterbox,
Though his teacher sets a barrier for him
His feet will tip over everything, even the Buddha.

My comment: Both answers miss the point by focussing upon the material and external. The chief monk says what the vase is not by reference to a physical object and uses words to do it ,(hence Mumon calls him "the chatterbox") despite the fact that he has been asked not to call its "name", i.e. use words to describe what it is or what it is not.

Isan shows that it is a water vase by revealing the contents. Hyakujo's question invites us to consider what the water vase is in its essence without words or name. Meditate on the essential nature of the water vase and become that water vase.

41. Bodhidharma Pacifies the Mind

Bodhidharma sits facing the wall. His future successor stands in the snow and presents his severed arm to Bodhidharma. He cries: "My mind is not pacified. Master, pacify my mind." Bodhidharma says: "If you bring me that mind, I will pacify it for you." The successor says: "When I search my mind I cannot hold it." Bodhidharma says: "Then your mind is pacified already."

Mumon's comment: That broken-toothed old Hindu, Bodhidharma, came thousands of miles over the sea from India to China as if he had something wonderful. He is like raising waves without wind. After he remained years in China he had only one disciple and that one lost his arm and was deformed. Alas, ever since he has had brainless disciples.

Why did Bodhidharma come to China?
For years monks have discussed this.
All the troubles that have followed since
Came from that teacher and disciple.

My comment: No-one, not even Bodhidharma can pacify someone else's mind. One can only pacify one's own mind. Therefore there are no teachers and disciples. Be your own disciple.

42. The Girl Comes Out from Meditation

In the time of Buddha Shakyamuni, Manjusri went to the assemblage of the Buddhas. When he arrived there, the conference was over and each Buddha had returned to his own Buddha-land. Only one girl was yet unmoved in deep meditation. Manjusri asked Buddha Shakyamuni how it was possible for this girl to reach this state, one which even he could not attain. "Bring her out from Samadhi and ask her yourself," said the Buddha. Manjusri walked around the girl three times and snapped his fingers. She still remained in meditation. So by his miracle power he transported her to a high heaven and tried his best to call her, but in vain. Buddha Shakyamuni said: "Even a hundred thousand Manjusris could not disturb her, but below this place, past twelve hundred million countries, is a Bodhisattva, Mo-myo, seed of delusion. If he comes here, she will awaken." No sooner had the Buddha spoken than that Bodhisattva sprang up from the earth and bowed and paid homage to the Buddha. Buddha directed him to arouse the girl. The Bodhisattva went in front of the girl and snapped his fingers, and in that instant the girl came out from her deep meditation.

Mumon's comment: Old Shakyamuni set a very poor stage. I want to ask you monks: If Manjusri, who is supposed to have been the teacher of seven Buddhas, could not bring this girl out of meditation, how then could a Bodhisattva who was a mere beginner? If you understand this intimately, you yourself can enter the great meditation while you are living in the world of delusion.

One could not awaken her, the other could.
Neither are good actors.
One wears the mask of god, one a devil's mask.
Had both failed, the drama still would be a comedy.

My comment: Manjusri operates from a spirit of envy: "how is it possible for this girl to be like this? Even I cannot attain this." She has passed beyond such concerns, so even a 100,000 Manjusris could not awaken her. The Bodhisattva in Mahayana Buddhism is a person on the road to enlightenment, who promises to assist others to find the way, because he longs for all sentient beings to find enlightenment. It is the unselfish compassion of Mo-myo which awakens the girl.

Jesus says: "Whoever would be great among you must be your servant, and whoever would be first among you must be slave of all. For the Son of Man came not to be served but to serve, and to give his life as a ransom for many." (Mark 10.43-45)

"A new commandment I give to you, that you love one another; even as I have loved you, that you also love one another. By this all people will know that you are my disciples, if you have love for one another." (John 13. 34-35)

43. Shuzan's Short Staff

Shuzan held out his short staff and said: "If you call this a short staff, you oppose its reality. If you do not call it a short staff, you ignore the fact. Now what do you wish to call this?"

Mumon's comment: If you call this a short staff, you oppose its reality. If you do not call it a short staff, you ignore the fact. It cannot be expressed with words and it cannot be expressed without words. Now say quickly what it is.

Holding out the short staff,
He gave an order of life or death.
Positive and negative interwoven,
Even Buddhas and patriarchs cannot escape this attack.

My comment: Calling the staff "short" makes it relative to something else, i.e. a longer staff. Calling it a "staff" is just a label, a word, a name, which tells us nothing about what Shuzan's staff is in its essence. Let the staff "be" what it is in itself.

Jesus says: "There will be more joy in heaven over one sinner who repents than over ninety-nine righteous persons who need no repentance." (Luke 15. 7)

My comment: Jesus deliberately uses the labels, "sinner" and "righteous" in order to challenge the assumptions made by labelling oneself and others in those terms. They tell us nothing about what the person is in their self. See also Luke 7. 36-50, where the woman labelled a "sinner" is praised by Jesus for her uninhibited love.

44. Basho's Staff

Basho said to his disciple: "When you have a staff, I will give it to you. If you have no staff, I will take it away from you."

Mumon's comment: When there is no bridge over the creek the staff will help me. When I return home on a moonless night the staff will accompany me. But if you call this a staff, you will enter hell like an arrow.

With this staff in my hand
I can measure the depths and shallows of the world.
The staff supports the heavens and makes firm the earth.
Everywhere it goes the true teaching will be spread.

My comment: Zen is about discovering and knowing what we already possess, rather than striving for what we do not have.

Jesus says: "To you it has been given to know the secrets of the kingdom of heaven, but to them it has not been given. For to him who has will more be given, and he will have in abundance; but from him who has not, even what he has will be taken away."

My comment: The key to the kingdom of heaven lies in accepting what has been given as pure gift, rather than in striving for more.

45. Who Is He?

Hoen said: "The past and future Buddhas, both are his servants. Who is he?"

Mumon's comment: If you realize clearly who he is, it is as if you met your own father on a busy street. There is no need to ask anyone whether or not your recognition is true.

Do not fight with another's bow and arrow.
Do not ride another's horse.
Do not discuss another's faults.
Do not interfere with another's work.

My comment: He is one's "true self." The goal of Zen is knowing oneself as if for the first time, not in comparison (either good or bad) with anyone else, but who you are in yourself. As T.S.Eliot says:

We shall not cease from exploration
And the end of all our exploring
Will be to arrive where we started
And know the place for the first time.
Through the unknown, remembered gate
When the last of earth left to discover
Is that which was the beginning;

Jesus says: "Woe to you, scribes and Pharisees, hypocrites! Because you shut people out of the kingdom of heaven; for you neither enter yourselves, nor allow those who would enter to go in." (Matthew 23. 13-14)

My comment: Jesus reserves his fiercest condemnation for those who are hypocritical and self-righteous and who therefore delude themselves and others by wearing a false mask instead of embracing their true self. This self-delusion closes the door to the kingdom of heaven.

46. Proceed from the Top of the Pole

Sekiso asked: "How can you proceed on from the top of a hundred-foot pole?" Another Zen teacher said: "One who sits on the top of a hundred-foot pole has attained a certain height but still is not handling Zen freely. He should proceed on from there and appear with his whole body in the ten parts of the world."

Mumon's comment: One can continue his steps or turn his body freely about on the top of the pole. In either case he should be respected. I want to ask you monks, however: How will you proceed from the top of that pole? Look out!

The man who lacks the third eye of insight
Will cling to the measure of the hundred feet.
Such a man will jump from there and kill himself,
Like a blind man misleading other blind men.

My comment: Zen bids us let go of all that we cling to. The pole represents all that we cling to. In order to discover oneself it is necessary to abandon all earthly security and be prepared to jump into the unknown.

Jesus says: " Everyone who has left houses, or brothers or sisters or father or mother or children or lands, for my name's sake, will receive a hundredfold, and inherit eternal life." (Matthew 19. 29)

"Blessed are you poor, for yours is the kingdom of God."
(Luke 6. 20)

47. Three Gates of Tosotsu

Tosotsu built three barriers and made the monks pass through them. The first barrier is studying Zen. In studying Zen the aim is to see one's own true nature. Now where is your true nature? Secondly, when one realizes his own true nature he will be free from birth and death. Now when you shut the light from your eyes and become a corpse, how can you free yourself? Thirdly, if you free yourself from birth and death, you should know where you are. Now your body separates into the four elements. Where are you?

Mumon's comment: Whoever can pass these three barriers will be a master wherever he stands. Whatever happens about him he will turn into Zen. Otherwise he will be living on poor food and not even enough of that to satisfy himself.

An instant realization sees endless time.
Endless time is as one moment.
When one comprehends the endless moment
He realizes the person who is seeing it.

My comment: The gates of Tosotsu are about freeing oneself from the restrictions of space and time and entering what Mumon refers to as the "endless moment." One's own true nature is eternal, "timeless."

Jesus says: "He who loves is life loses it, and he who hates his life in this world will keep it for eternal life." (John 12. 25) "God so loved the world that he gave his only Son, that whoever believes in him should not perish, but have eternal life."

My comment: For "eternal" think "timeless", rather than "everlasting."

48. One Road of Kembo

A Zen pupil asked Kembo: "All Buddhas of the ten parts of the universe enter the one road of Nirvana. Where does that road begin?" Kembo, raising his walking stick and drawing the figure one in the air, said: "Here it is." This pupil went to Ummon and asked the same question. Ummon, who happened to have a fan in his hand, said: "This fan will reach to the thirty-third heaven and hit the nose of the presiding deity there. It is like the Dragon Carp of the Eastern Sea tipping over the rain-cloud with his tail."

Mumon's comment: One teacher enters the deep sea and scratches the earth and raises dust. The other goes to the mountain top and raises waves that almost touch heaven. One holds, the other gives out. Each supports the profound teaching with a single hand. Kembo and Ummon are like two riders neither of whom can surpass the other. It is very difficult to find the perfect man. Frankly, neither of them know where the road starts.

Before the first step is taken the goal is reached.
Before the tongue is moved the speech is finished.
More than brilliant intuition is needed
To find the origin of the right road.

My comment: The road to Nirvana begins right here where you are. It also begins in the highest heaven. Both meet at the same point – highest heaven is right here where you are. The "origin of the right road" has to be found in ourselves.

Jesus says: "Preach as you go, saying, 'The kingdom of heaven is at hand.' (Matthew 10. 7) "Truly, truly I say to you, you will see heaven opened, and the angels of God ascending and descending upon the Son of Man." (John 1. 51)

"I am the way and the truth and the life." (John 14. 6)

My comment: The kingdom of heaven is right here. The way to the kingdom of heaven starts here. We do not need to search for truth or life or the way to the Father, we already have it in ourselves. Jesus has come to show us the way, to be the way, that we might see the heaven opened right where we are.

49. Amban's Addition

Amban, a layman Zen student, said: "Mu-mon has just published forty-eight koans and called the book Gateless Gate. He criticizes the old patriarchs' words and actions. I think he is very mischievous. He is like an old doughnut seller trying to catch a passerby to force his doughnuts down his mouth. The customer can neither swallow nor spit out the doughnuts, and this causes suffering. Mu-mon has annoyed everyone enough, so I think I shall add one more as a bargain. I wonder if he himself can eat this bargain. If he can, and digest it well, it will be fine, but if not, we will have to put it back into the frying pan with his forty-eight also and cook them again. Mu-mon, you eat first, before someone else does: "Buddha, according to a sutra, once said: 'Stop, stop. Do not speak. The ultimate truth is not even to think.'"

Amban's comment: Where did that so-called teaching come from? How is it that one could not even think it? Suppose someone spoke about it then what became of it? Buddha himself was a great chatterbox and in this sutra spoke contrarily. Because of this, persons like Mu-mon appear afterwards in China and make useless doughnuts, annoying people. What shall we do after all? I will show you. Then Amban put his palms together, folded his hands, and said: "Stop, stop. Do not speak. The ultimate truth is not even to think. And now I will make a little circle on the sutra with my finger and add that five thousand other sutras and Vimalakirti's gateless gate all are here!"

If anyone tells you fire is light,
Pay no attention.
When two thieves meet they need no introduction:
They recognize each other without question.

My comment: Amban adds a caution at the close of Mumon's book of words. He points us to the word which ends all words, the sutra which cancels all sutras. Buddha's sutra is contradictory. The phrase, "according to a sutra," contradicts what the sutra says; that ultimate truth goes beyond words, thoughts or concepts.

Jesus says: "The wind blows wherever it pleases. You hear its sound, but you cannot tell where it comes from or where it is going. So it is with everyone born of the Spirit." (John 3. 8)

My comment: How tempting it has been for Christians down the ages to try to package and claim monopoly on the Holy Spirit. Jesus rather bids us recognise the sound of the Spirit, wherever it may be found, for the life of the Spirit goes beyond our imagining and understanding. There is no last word, the future is always open.........!

Here ends the commentary on the Mumonkan, the Gateless Gate or 49 essential koans of Zen Buddhism. I am now also adding a few other classic Zen stories, mostly of a later date, some of which contain koans or have the character of koans.

Some Classic Zen Stories

A Cup of Tea

Nan-in, a Japanese master during the Meiji era (1868-1912), received a university professor who came to inquire about Zen.

Nan-in served tea. He poured his visitor's cup full, and then kept on pouring.

The visitor watched the overflow until he no longer could restrain himself. "It is overfull. No more will go in!"

"Like this cup," Nan-in said, "you are full of your own opinions and speculations. How can I show you Zen unless you first empty your cup."

My comment: It is possible to be so full of words, concepts, ideas, speculations, theories, doctrines that all these things become security objects to which we cling, rather than face the emptiness of not knowing. However, they prevent us from being empty and receptive.

I am reminded of the author of the English medieval classic, "The Cloud of Unknowing", who wrote:

"When you first begin, you find only darkness, and as it were a cloud of unknowing. You don't know what this means except that in your will you feel a simple steadfast intention reaching out towards God. Do what you will, this darkness and this cloud remain between you and God, and stop you from seeing him in the clear light of rational understanding, and from experiencing his loving sweetness in your affection. Reconcile yourself to wait in this darkness as long as is necessary, but still go on longing after him whom you love...Strike that thick cloud of unknowing with the sharp dart of longing love, and on no account whatever think of giving up."

Sit patiently with an empty cup,
Wait patiently for it to be filled.
Out of your emptiness
Will flow streams of living water.

Jesus says: "Ask and it will be given to you; seek and you will find; knock and it will be opened to you." (Matthew 6. 7)

The Moon cannot be stolen

Ryokan, a Zen master, lived the simplest kind of life in a little hut at the foot of a mountain. On evening a thief visited the hut only to discover that there was nothing in it to steal.

Ryokan returned and caught him. "You may have come a long way to visit me," he told the prowler, "and you should not return empty-handed. Please take my clothes as a gift." The thief was bewildered. He took the clothes and slunk away.

Ryokan sat naked, watching the moon. "Poor fellow," he mused, "I wish I could give him this beautiful moon."

My comment: As well as clinging to words and concepts, we also cling on to material things, possessions, as a source of security. Because of this, we find it hard to be generous. What do we treasure above all, which has the eternal quality of Ryokan's moon?

How can I give the gift of the moon,
How can I give the timeless gift of eternity?
It is not mine to give,
But others can receive it.

Jesus says: "Do not lay up for yourselves treasure on earth, where moth and rust consume and where thieves break in and steal, but lay up for yourselves treasures in heaven...For where you treasure is, there will your heart be also." (Matthew 6. 19)

"If any one would sue you and take your coat, let him have your cloak as well." (Matthew 5. 40)

Muddy Road

Tanzan and Ekido were once travelling together down a muddy road. A heavy rain was falling.

Coming around a bend, they met a lovely girl in a silk kimono and sash, unable to cross the intersection.

"Come on, girl," said Tanzan at once. Lifting her in his arms, he carried her over the mud.

Ekido didn't speak again until that night when they reached a lodging temple. Then he no longer could restrain himself. "We monks don't go near females," he told Tanzan, "especially not young and lovely ones. It is dangerous. Why did you do that?"

"I left the girl there," said Tanzan. "Are you still carrying her?"

My comment: In contrasting the two characters, one of the key phrases, which opens a window onto the personality of Ekido, is "He could no longer restrain himself." Tanzan demonstrates his Zen by his detachment, which enables him to give assistance without fear of being distracted. Ekido cannot remain detached; he cannot restrain his mind from dwelling upon the girl and transfers his frustration by berating Tanzan. Detachment is not about removing oneself from the world, but about not allowing it to influence who you are in yourself.

The one observes, assists and leaves behind,
The other chases after her in his mind.
Removing oneself from temptation
Never solves the problem.

What they said about Jesus: "When the Pharisee who had invited Jesus saw it, he said to himself, "If this man were a prophet, he would have known who and what sort of woman this is who is touching him, for she is a sinner." (Luke 7. 39)

The Sound of One Hand

The master of Kennin temple was Mokurai, Silent Thunder. He had a little protégé named Toyo, who was only twelve years old. Toyo saw the older disiples visit the master's room each morning and evening to receive instructions in sanzen or peesonal guidance in which they were given koans to stop mind-wandering.

Toyo wished to do sanzen also.

"Wait a while," said Mokurai. "You are too young."

But the child insisted, so the teacher finally consented.

Ij the evening little Toyo went at the proper time to the threshold of Mokurai's sanzen room. He struck the gong to announce his presence, bowed respectfully outside the door, and went to sit before the master in respectful silence.

"You can hear the sound of two hands when they clap together," said Mokurai. "Now show me the sound of one hand."

Toyo bowed and went to his room to consider the problem. From his window he could hear the music of the geishas. "Ah! I have it!" he proclaimed.

The next evening, when his teacher asked him to illustrate the sound of one hand, Toyo began to play the music of the geishas.

"No, no," said Mokurai. "That will never do. That is not the sound of one hand. You have not got it at all."

Thinking that such music might interrupt, Toyo moved his abode to a quiet place. He meditated again. "What can the sound of one hand be?" He happened to hear some water dripping. "I have it," imagined Toyo.

When he next appeared before his teacher, Toyo imitated dripping water.

"What is that?" asked Mokurai. "That is the sound of dripping water, but not the sound of one hand. Try again."

In vain Toyo meditated to hear the sound of one hand. He heard the sighing of the wind. But the sound was rejected. He heard the cry of an owl. This also was refused.

The sound of one hand was not the locusts.

For more than ten times, Toyo visited Mokurai with different sounds. All were wrong. For almost a year he pondered what the sound of one hand might be.

At last little Toyo entered true meditation and transcended all sounds. "I could collect no more," he explained later, "so I reached the soundless sound."

Toyo had realised the sound of one hand.

My comment: The sound of one hand was given by master Hakuin as an introductory koan, an alternative to meditating upon "Mu" (See Mumonkan 1 – Joshu's Dog). This story is a commentary on the koan in itself. Like Mu, it is necessary to become the one hand in order to hear its sound.

Beyond all forms, beyond all thoughts,
Beyond all sounds in the world around
The canvas on which all other sounds are painted.
Is the soundless sound.

Open Your Own Treasure House

Daiju visited the master Baso in China. Baso asked: "What do you seek?"

"Enlightenment," replied Daiju.

"You have your own treasure house. Why do you search outside?" Baso asked.

Daiju inquired: "Where is my treasure house?"

Baso answered, "What you are asking is your treasure house."

Daiju was enlightened! Ever after he urged his friends: "Open your own treasure house and use those treasures."

My comment: As with Mumonkan 39 (Ummon's sidetrack), there can be no second-hand Zen. One has to be oneself and discover one's own treasure house.

Why search outside
When the truth lies within.
Diligently follow the path, which leads
To your own treasure house.

Jesus says: "Every scribe who has been trained for the kingdom of heaven is like a householder who brings out of his treasure what is old and what is new." (Matthew 13. 52)

No water, No Moon.

When the nun Chiyono studied Zen under Bukko of Engaku, she was unable to attain the fruits of meditation for a long time.

At last one moonlit night she was carrying water in an old pail bound with bamboo. The bamboo broke and the bottom fell out of the pail. At that moment Chiyono was set free!

In commemoration she wrote a poem:

> In this way and that I tried to save the old pail.
> Since the bamboo strip was weakening and about to break
> Until at last the bottom fell out.
> No more water in the pail!
> No more moon in the water!

My comment: Chiyono was studying Zen. Studying will get her nowhere. Dropping the old pail is letting go of her "mind." Until that moment she has been wasting her time looking at reflections in the water, a reflected moon rather than the true moon. The mind reflects and distorts reality. Enlightenment comes to Chiyono suddenly, like an accident. It is a gift of grace. It impossible to embrace the truth unless we are prepared to let go of all our previous knowledge and expectations. It is when Chiyono is left empty-handed that she is enlightened.

Jesus says: "Take heed, watch; for you do not know when the time will come."(Mark 13. 33)

My comment: We need to be ready and receptive for the "accident" of grace to happen.

Black-Nosed Buddha

A nun who was searching for enlightenment made a statue of Buddha and covered it with gold leaf. Wherever she went she carried this golden Buddha with her.

Years passed and, still carrying her Buddha, the nun came to live in a small temple in the country where there were many Buddhas, each one with its own particular shrine.

The nun wished to burn incense before her golden Buddha. Not liking the idea of the perfume straying to others, she devised a funnel through which the smoke would ascend only to her statue. This blackened the nose of the golden Buddha, making it especially ugly.

My comment: You may not be able to have second-hand Zen, but nor can you have your own personal Buddha. She thinks by carrying her personal Buddha that she has found the Buddha. Ultimately, her possessiveness becomes both a burden and an ugly distortion of her "search for enlightenment." The story reminds us how religion can become self-indulgent and exclusive, which in the end makes a monster idol out of what we adore.

Jesus says: "Believe me, the hour is coming when neither on this mountain nor in Jerusalem will you worship the Father...the hour is coming and now is, when true worshippers will worship the Father in spirit and truth." (John 4. 21,23)

The Gates of Paradise

A soldier named Nobushige came to Hakuin and asked: "Is there really a paradise and a hell?"

"Who are you?" inquired Hakuin.

"I am a samurai," the warrior replied.

"You, a soldier!" exclaimed Hakuin. "What kind of ruler would have you as his guard? Your face looks like that of a beggar."

Nobushige became so angry that he began to draw his sword, but Hakuin continued: "So, you have a sword! Your weapon is probably much too dull to cut off my head."

As Nobushige drew his sword, Hakuin remarked: "Here open the gates of hell!"

At these words the samurai, perceiving the master's discipline, sheathed his sword and bowed.

"Here open the gates of paradise," said Hakuin.

My comment: the samurai queried the objective existence of heaven and hell, but reveals by his behaviour that heaven and hell are of our own choice and making. His greatest weakness is his pride, his puffed-up false image, which both causes him to open up the gates of hell of his anger and also prevents him from ever knowing his true self.

Jesus says: He who is greatest among you shall be your servant; whoever exalts himself will be humbled, and whoever humbles himself will be exalted." (Matthew 23. 11,12)

A Letter to a Dying Man

Bassui wrote the following letter to one of his disciples who was about to die:
"The essence of your mind is not born, so it will never die. It is not an existence, which is perishable. It is not an emptiness, which is a mere void. It has neither colour nor form. It enjoys no pleasures and suffers no pains.
I know you are very ill. Like a good Zen student, you are facing that sickness squarely. You may not know exactly who is suffering, but question yourself: What is the essence of this mind? Think only of this. You will need no more. Covet nothing. Your end which is endless is as a snowflake dissolving in the pure air."

My comment: This story contains something of the true essence of Zen; namely a detachment, a readiness to "let go" and embrace the transitory nature of life, so that the present moment is timeless and eternal.

Jesus says: "Father, into your hands I commend my spirit." (Luke 23. 46)

"The Way to Buddhahood is easy. They who do not perpetrate evil, they who do not try to grasp at life or death but work for the good of all living things with utter compassion, giving respect to those older and loving understanding to those younger than themselves, they who do not reject, search for, think on or worry about anything have the name of Buddha: you must look for nothing more."
(Master Dogen)

"Everyone who hears these words of mine and does them will be like a wise man who built his house upon the rock."
(Jesus)

Lightning Source UK Ltd.
Milton Keynes UK
UKOW07f1220200115

244779UK00001B/18/P